A GUIDE TO PLANNING AND CRUISING

THE GREAT CIRCLE ROUTE

AROUND THE EASTERN USA

BY

G. BICKLEY REMMEY, JR.

REVISED AND UPDATED BY

LAURA CANNELL

Paradise Cay Publications, Inc.
Arcata, California

The text of this book is composed in Minion Display font.

ISBN 0-939837-68-4, 978-0-939837-68-4

Cover design by Rob Johnson, www.johnsondesign.org
Editing and book design by Linda Scantlebury www.we-edit.com
Printed in the United States.

Photos by G. Bickley Remmey, Jr.

Published by
Paradise Cay Publications, Inc.
P. O. Box 29
Arcata, CA 95518-0029
website: www.paracay.com   e-mail: info@paracay.com
(800) 736-4509   (707) 822-9063   (707) 822-9163 fax

DISCLAIMER

This information is for planning purposes only. Be aware that the navigable waterways described in this book constantly change. Vessels should always be equipped with up-to-date charts of their intended route. Mariners should also keep abreast of chart changes as posted in the Notices to Mariners.

Every effort has been made to ensure that each entry is complete and accurate; however, the authors and publisher assume no responsibility and disclaim any liability for any injury or damage resulting from the use or effect of any product or information specified in this publication.

PUBLISHER'S FOREWORD

In 1999 Bick Remmey first published *A Planning and Cruising Guide to The Great Circle Cruise Around the Eastern USA* as a record of his 1996/97 Great Circle voyage in *Nittany Navy,* a 36-foot Carver aft-cabin motor yacht, with his wife Jeri. Although it remains an interesting account of the voyage, much of Bick's book had become outdated in the intervening nine years.

In order to revise and update the book to make it suitable for use by today's mariner, Paradise Cay employed the services of Laura Cannell of Marine Navigation, Inc., Lisa Morehouse of Paradise Cay, Inc., and Linda Scantlebury of We-Edit. Without the services of these three people, this book would not have seen the light of day.

Laura provided invaluable expertise to update and correct Bick's original work. Please see Laura's biography, which appears on the back cover and on page *vii.* Throughout the book, Laura's comments are set out in grayed boxes. If in any instance her comments conflict with the original, it is the publisher's advice that Laura's recommendations be followed.

Lisa Morehouse contacted all of the marinas to update information about their facilities, address, phone number, website, and so forth. Any marinas that no longer exist were left out.

The task of pulling together these many pieces and of editing, designing, and formatting the book fell to Linda Scantlebury of We-Edit.

As publisher, I thank all those who contributed to this work. I believe it is now a fine reference for anyone wishing to take this voyage.

Matt Morehouse, Publisher

ABOUT G. BICKLEY REMMEY, JR.

Bick Remmey got a late start in cruising, having begun in 1989 at the age of 54 with the purchase of *Fanta-Sea*, a 27-foot Carver Express cruiser. Based out of Avalon, New Jersey, over the next four years Bick and Jeri Remmey cruised to Washington, D.C., to North Carolina, and on four occasions to the Chesapeake.

In 1994 the Remmeys purchased *Nittany Navy*, a 36-foot Carver aft-cabin motor yacht, which was ideal for two couples, since it had staterooms at opposite ends of the boat, each stateroom with its own head. In 1994 and 1995 the Remmeys made another two Chesapeake trips plus a 1,250-mile round trip to Montreal, Canada. On each of these voyages, four people were aboard.

Along with their cruising experience, Bick and Jeri both took the U. S. Power Squadron Public Boating and Seamanship courses. Bick also took the piloting and advanced piloting courses, and in 1993 he got his captain's license from the U. S. Coast Guard.

The Remmeys started their Great Circle Cruise in June, 1996; they completed the Great Circle in July, 1997.

ABOUT LAURA CANNELL

Laura Cannell owns Marine Navigation, Inc. (located in La Grange, Illinois, a suburb of Chicago), a large source of navigation aids.

As a chart agent—a licensed distributor of charts made by various government agencies for both domestic and international waters—Laura deals with clients from around the world. Since 1984 her clients have turned to her for personalized boating advice, as well as to buy cruising guides, classic texts, navigation aids, and supplies.

CONTENTS

AUTHOR'S VOYAGES

PREPARATION

CRUISING THE GREAT CIRCLE ROUTE

CHAPTER 1

CHOICES

If the idea of taking the longest one-way inland cruise possible in the United States (approximately 5 , 4 0 0 miles) appeals to you, then read on. This longest inland cruise includes the Atlantic Intracoastal waterway, the Erie Canal, the Great Lakes, the Mississippi River, the Gulf Intracoastal Waterway, and the Florida Keys. This voyage allows you to see the United States in a very different way from traveling on land or in the air.

Most people who make this trip are retired or take a year off from work. However, we took the trip and I'm not retired and I didn't take a year off. Passage time varies from 18 weeks (I don't think you would want to do it any faster) to one year, depending upon the speed of your vessel and the amount of time you choose to stay at each port. Most of the people whom we met doing the Great Circle cruise were from Florida and were doing the trip in six months. Typically, they left Florida on the first of May and returned home at the end of October. People who take a year to do the trip usually spend the entire winter in Florida and/or the Bahamas.

We did the trip in 18 weeks spread over 57 weeks. Our first leg was Avalon, New Jersey to Chicago, which took 6 weeks (June 7 to July 16, 1996). The second leg was Chicago to New Orleans in 4 weeks

(September 9 to October 7, 1996). The third leg was New Orleans to West Palm Beach in 5 weeks (January 17 to February 22, 1997), and the last leg was West Palm Beach to Avalon, New Jersey in 3 weeks (June 15 to July 11, 1997). In other words, in 1996 we cruised for 10 weeks, and in 1997 we cruised for 8 weeks.

Your first major decision is when to make the trip. It isn't necessary to wait until you are retired or until your children grow up. One couple that I heard about took their children out of school (2nd grade and 7th grade) for a year, and the children's mother, a schoolteacher, tutored them in their respective grades with an approved correspondence course for the year of their cruise.

I first started thinking about making the trip in 1991, and I then assumed that we would make the trip in the year 2000 after I retired at age 65. At the time, we had a 27-foot Carver Express cruiser that we kept at our shore house in Avalon, New Jersey and took once a year to the Chesapeake for a two-week cruise. It was fun to dream about the big cruise around the Eastern United States.

Once I got serious about the trip, I realized I would need to know more about boating and navigation. I was already a member of the U.S. Power Squadron, so I signed up for their navigation courses, piloting and advanced piloting, which were very helpful. In January 1993 I passed the Coast Guard exam for my captain's license.

A lot of factors go into that first major decision of when to make the trip. If you are retired and have the right boat, you are ready to go. However, if you are not retired, you must decide how much time to take off (18 weeks to a year) and when you can do that. I guess for most people the easiest time to take the trip would be their first year of retirement. However, if you have an interest in taking your children out of school and offering them an adventure like this, you probably will never regret the decision.

The time between deciding you want to take the trip and when the trip starts can be lots of fun. For us, this period was 5 years, 1991 to 1996. We spent three years going to boat shows to find the right boat. After we decided on the exact boat we wanted for the trip, we had to find one on sale, since we had decided to buy a used boat to save money. In June of 1994 we found the boat and bought it. Since our whole family had graduated from Penn State (my wife and I plus our three sons), we named the boat *Nittany Navy.*

In July 1995 we took the *Nittany Navy* on a 1,250-mile, three-week inland cruise from Avalon, New Jersey (near Cape May) to Montreal, Canada and back. Besides providing us with a wonderful vacation, this trip prepared us for the big trip in a number of ways. We learned about locks (60 of them). We learned that we needed a backup GPS for the Loran, and that we needed 100 feet of hose. We spent the fall of 1995 and spring of 1996 getting charts and cruising guides, planning our detailed itinerary, and getting all of our guest crew members organized.

Once you have decided when you are going on the trip, the next important decision is how many people will be on board—usually one, two, three, or four. This decision will determine what size boat you take. Obviously, if you are doing the trip single-handed, the boat could be quite small. Most people make the trip with two. However, we did most of the trip with a crew of four. Our crew mostly consisted of my wife and I, plus another couple who shared a week or 10 days with us. In total we had thirteen different crews.

One can make the voyage in a sailboat, but that is not the ideal type of boat for this trip. During most of the inland portion of the trip, the mast would have to be taken down and put into a horizontal trestle to permit the sailboat to get under hundreds of low bridges. The maximum boat height above the waterline for this trip is 19 feet—15.5 feet the way we went. This means that a sailboat would have to make most of the trip under power. Also, the draft of a sailboat is a problem. A trawler is probably the most economical type boat for this trip; however, the mast will have to be hinged to get under the 19-foot limit. A sport fisherman or convertible can be used, so long as the height stays under 19 feet. Most express cruisers will not have a height problem even though they can be quite large.

We chose an aft cabin motor yacht because it maximized the living space and was ideal for two couples, with a stateroom and head at opposite ends of the boat. Our boat was 16 feet 3 inches high to the top of the radome, with an overall length of 42 feet, a 14-foot beam, and a 37-inch draft.

Another important consideration is gas versus diesel. Since gas engines are much cheaper to buy and diesel engines are cheaper to run, the best choice depends on a number of factors. If your normal boating use is less than 100 hours per year, not counting this trip, you probably are better off with gas. If your normal boating use is over 100 hours per year, diesel could be justified. This trip is approximately 360 hours run time when cruising at 18 knots and averaging 15 mph including slow areas. The same trip is 720 hours when cruising at 7.5 knots. Our average seasonal usage cruising around the Chesapeake was 80 hours, so we chose gas.

> Although the author made his voyage in a gas-powered boat, most experts would advise choosing a twin-screw diesel-powered vessel with a range of at least 200 miles. This becomes even more important in the high fuel price environment.

Once you have decided on the size of the boat, the style of the boat, and the type of power, you are ready to start shopping. The next decision is new or used. New boats have the advantage that you order them just the way you want them and they have new engines. Used boats cost a lot less. We bought a four-year-old boat that looked like new but had 500 hours on the engines and did not have an aft deck enclosure, which we wanted. We added the aft deck enclosure to make the boat just the way we would have ordered it, and the savings over the price of a new boat were still substantial.

The economics of this trip can vary substantially. A 40-foot single-engine diesel trawler cruising at 7 knots could do the entire trip with as little as 2,000 gallons of fuel. Cruising at 18 knots most of the time, we used about 9,000 gallons of gas. If we had cruised at 10 mph as we did in the Erie Canal, we would have used only 5,000 gallons for the whole trip. If we had kept our 27-foot boat, we would have also used much less fuel. In other words, the amount of fuel you use depends not only on the size of your boat but also on how fast you run. If you are going to take a year to do the trip, it makes sense to cruise at slower speeds and save fuel.

The next major cost is staying in marinas versus anchoring out. In 1996 the average cost in a marina was $1.00 per foot per night. (It was $2.00 per foot in 2006.) Our boat is 36 feet at the waterline, so in 1996 we paid an average of $36.00 per night. If you anchor out, your only cost is the fuel to run the generator ($2 to $10 per night, 1996 prices) for air conditioning, lights, and so forth.

Another major variable is eating in restaurants or cooking on board. We ate breakfast and lunch on board and almost always ate dinner in a restaurant. If you cook on board, it obviously costs a lot less.

If you compare anchoring out and cooking aboard a 40-foot trawler with a single-diesel engine that usually cruises at 7 knots, to eating out and staying in marinas with a 40-foot gas-powered motor yacht usually cruising at 20 knots, you will find that the total cost for two people could vary from $50 to $250 per day or more. Therefore, the cost of the trip depends on the choices you make.

In summation, here are the choices you must make:

1. When to take the trip.
2. How long the trip shall be (18 weeks to a year).
3. How many people on board.
4. What size boat you need.

CHAPTER 2

THE ROUTE

Where you start and end the cruise depends on where you live. The route passes through or borders 20 states plus Ontario, Canada. People from New England can join the cruise at New York. People from the upper Midwest can join the cruise at St. Louis from the upper Mississippi River or the Missouri River.

The cruise passes through the following major cities:

New York	St. Louis	Jacksonville
Buffalo	Mobile	Savannah
Cleveland	New Orleans	Charleston
Detroit	Tampa	Norfolk
Chicago	Miami	Baltimore

It could easily include:

Toronto
Milwaukee
Philadelphia
Washington, DC

As previously stated, where you start and end the cruise depends on where you live. The map on the cover shows the entire route. The most popular direction to go is counterclockwise because most of the river currents, including the Mississippi River, flow that way. Also, the prevailing winds on the gulf are west to east. It is possible to go clockwise; however, a trawler that cruises at 7 knots would have difficulty bucking a 5- to 6-knot current in the Mississippi. This book assumes that the route is counterclockwise.

The timing of the trip depends on where you start. The Erie Canal is closed from early November to late April, depending on weather. In 1996 the Canal did not open until early June because of high water levels from spring rains. Since half the trip is in fresh water, ice is a problem in the winter and early spring. Therefore, the Erie Canal and the Great Lakes should be transited in summer. Assuming you stick with the two rules of "counterclockwise" and "Erie Canal and Great Lakes only in the summer," the timing for your trip will be determined by your starting point. The following are some examples:

STARTING POINT	BEGIN
New York	June
Chicago	September
New Orleans	February
Miami	April

One of the great things about this trip is that it is a leisurely sightseeing tour of the Eastern United States, which is the reason that it is almost entirely on inland waterways. The only times when the cruise is not on an inland waterway are:

1. Cape May, New Jersey to New York Harbor. Run 2 miles off shore
    in Atlantic Ocean for 150 miles.

2. Carrabelle, Florida to Tarpon Springs, Florida—180 miles across
    the Gulf—can be done in two days. First day Carrabelle to Cedar
    Key, Florida (1 2 0 miles) and second day Cedar Key to Tarpon
    Springs (60 miles).

> **Cedar Key not recommended. No fuel, too shallow,
> no supplies or services. Note: This is the area Bick
> went aground.**

3. Marco Island to Key West. 98 miles across the Gulf.

4. Key West to Marathon. Run outside in the ocean for 43 miles, re-
    entering Intracoastal waterway at Marathon.

Note: Passages 3 and 4 above are eliminated if you take the Okeechobee
waterway from the west coast of Florida to the east coast.

There is a variation in the route that depends on the height of
your boat. If your boat is 15 feet 6 inches or less, you can stay on the
Erie Canal all the way to Buffalo. However, if your height above the
waterline is between 15 feet 6 inches and 19 feet (maximum height for
this trip), you must take the Erie Canal to Oswego, New York on Lake
Ontario. From Oswego you cruise west on Lake Ontario to the Welland
Canal, which connects into Lake Erie near Buffalo. Allow a full day to
go through the Welland Canal System, because the large commercial
boats (1,000 feet long) traveling on the Saint Lawrence Seaway have the
right of way and it is not uncommon for pleasure boats to wait hours
at each lock.

Overhead clearances for the inland portion of the Great Circle Trip are often misstated. Bridge heights in *Coast Pilot* tabulations are rounded down to lower number. Listed in the *US Great Lakes Coast Pilot #6*, the 19-foot Illinois Central Gulf Railroad Bridge (mile 300.6 on chart) in Lemont, IL on the Illinois Waterway System is the lowest fixed clearance and cannot be avoided. On the N.Y.S.C.S. (New York State Canal System): Minimum vertical clearance at Maximum Navigable Pool Level under bridges and gates along: Champlain**, Cayuga & Seneca Canal and the Erie Canal west of Three River is 15-1/2 feet; Oswego Canal and the Erie Canal east of Three Rivers is 20 feet.

** Depending upon local conditions this clearance could be as much as 17 feet.

You will note that the route only spends 217 miles on the Mississippi and then goes 46 miles up the Ohio River to the Tennessee River. This route, called the Tenn-Tom, is a parallel route to the Mississippi to get to the Gulf. The Tenn-Tom route was opened in 1985 when a canal system was completed that connected the Tennessee River with the Tombigbee River to provide an alternate route to the Mississippi. The lower Mississippi, being mainly a barge river, is relatively unfriendly for pleasure boats. There are long distances (200 miles) between gas stops; marinas are few and far between. The barge traffic is very heavy and the swift current often carries large debris such as telephone poles. By comparison the Tenn-Tom is tranquil, there is very little current, there is much less barge traffic, and gas stops and marinas are less than 100 miles apart. The Tenn-Tom is also very scenic.

> The main reason most pleasure craft travel the Tombigbee is it offers amenities. Some cruisers prefer the Lower Mississippi because transit time is quicker and there are no locks to contend with; however, services are scarce.

As you can see on the route map, the Tenn-Tom brings you into the gulf at Mobile, Alabama, which means that you have to backtrack 160 miles to get to New Orleans. On the other hand, the Mississippi goes right to New Orleans. Staying on the Mississippi would be faster—especially with a slow boat—because of the swift current. A boat with a range of 300 miles or more would not have a fuel problem; however, you would have to anchor out sometimes, and it can be hard to find moorings out of the current with sufficient depth. The main reason most people prefer the Tenn-Tom to the lower Mississippi is that it avoids the swift current and the large floating debris problem.

Another route option is the Okeechobee waterway that goes from Fort Myers on the west coast of Florida to Stuart on the east coast. By taking this route you must backtrack to visit South Florida and the Keys.

Here are your route choices:

1. Lake Ontario and the Welland Canal versus the western half of the Erie Canal.

2. The lower Mississippi River versus the Tenn-Tom waterway.

3. The Okeechobee waterway versus sailing directly to Key West from Naples.

Alternate routes:

From Hudson River travel north on the Champlain Canal through Lake Champlain to Riviere Richelieu to St. Lawrence River to Lake Ontario

or

Ottawa River to Rideau Waterway to Lake Ontario to the Trent Severn Waterway to Georgian Bay and North Channel of Lake Huron through the Straits of Mackinac to Lake Michigan.

CHAPTER 3

PLANNING

We spent many, many hours over a two-year period planning this trip. Therefore, one of the main purposes of this book is to simplify the planning for others. The steps involved in planning the trip are as follows:

1. Buy all the cruising guides listed below. All can be ordered from Marine Navigation, Inc. Prices are for 2006.

    Waterway Guide
    To order call 800-233-3359 or Marine Navigation, Inc.
    Price:
    - _Waterway Guide—Great Lakes_ $39.95
      Includes route south to Gulf of Mexico
    - _Waterway Guide—Northern_ $39.95
      C & D Canal to Erie Canal
    - _Waterway Guide—Southern_ $39.95
      New Orleans to Jacksonville, Florida
    - _Waterway Guide—Mid-Atlantic_ $39.95
      Jacksonville, Florida to C & D Canal

    Lakeland Boating
    To order call 800-589-9491 or Marine Navigation, Inc.

- *Ports O'Call Lake Ontario* $35.95
     New edition due early 2006
- *Ports O'Call Lake Erie & St. Clair* $44.95
     Buffalo to Port Huron
- *Ports O'Call Lake Huron* $44.95
     Port Huron to Mackinac Island
- *Ports O'Call Lake Michigan* $44.95
     Mackinac Island to Chicago

The Waterways Journal
- *Quimby's Cruising Guide* $39.00
     Chicago to Mobile, AL.
     To order call 314-241-7354 or Marine Navigation, Inc.

2. Determine the time frame for the trip. This includes the overall length of the trip as well as the starting date. You will recall in Chapter 2 we discussed the fact that the starting date depends on where you live.

3. Determine the average number of miles per day that you would like to cover when cruising. This will depend on the speed of your boat and the number of hours you wish to run. We averaged 15 miles per hour and I like to run about 5 hours, so I used 75 miles per day for planning. (To average 15 miles per hour we cruised at 17 knots.) Actually our run times varied from as little as one hour to a maximum of 10 hours on several occasions.

Speed is restricted in many areas of this trip. Speed limit and no-wake zones are not always marked. The prudent mariner must be alert and recognize these areas.

4.   Using the cruising guides, select the ports close to your daily range. Once you have selected the ports using the cruising guides, you can select the marina and/or anchorage where you would like to stay. The guides list detailed information on each marina in a port area. To select a marina, I first checked to see if they offered transient slips. Next, I checked to see if they had gas, then 50-amp electricity, then a restaurant. For two-day layovers, I also looked to see if they had laundry facilities. If you choose to anchor out instead of renting a slip, the cruising guides are excellent sources for anchorage locations. All the marinas where we stayed are listed in Chapters 5 through 17, along with a list of their services. I would stay at these same marinas again. The marinas listed are not necessarily the ones we originally selected. As we traveled and talked to people we met, they recommended marinas in areas they were familiar with, and if these were different than the marinas I had selected, I changed to the one recommended.

5.   Write an itinerary that lists the dates, ports, and distances. This is your master cruising plan. I would suggest planning a one-day layover every four or five days to do laundry. I would also suggest assuming you would have to stay one day per week in port because of bad weather. This means that, exclusive of sightseeing days, you would plan to cruise no more than 5 days per week. Using our situation as an example, we could have done the 5,400 mile trip at 75 miles per day in 72 days total. We actually did the trip in 125 days, which I think is a minimum. If I were retired, I would have taken more time, perhaps 180 days.

Most boaters plan to take advantage of sightseeing, current local events, and history. I suggest they request literature (well in advance of their trip) from the local Chamber of Commerce along their planned route. Also very important in preplanning is to make sure insurance coverage is in effect for various portions of the trip, such as hurricane season (June 1 through November 30) in the Gulf of Mexico and Atlantic Ocean.

For a detailed description of the complete route as actually traveled by the author—including waterways, facilities, and locks—see Appendix A.

CHAPTER 4

OUTFITTING THE BOAT

This chapter covers the special things you will need on your boat for the Great Circle Route. This chapter does not list all the standard things that every boat should have, such as life preservers, flares, a compass, and so on.

1. Charts

I purchased charts for the trip in December 1995, at which time electronic charts were not as detailed and were much more expensive than standard charts. I realize that electronic charts are better and cheaper; however, the charts listed here are all standard charts.

Individual NOAA charts purchased separately are usually more expensive. It is more economical to buy charts in the form of chart books, if available. Boat/US offers discounted prices on chart books covering the Great Lakes and the coastal areas.

Charts available from Boat/US or Marine Navigation, Inc.
To order, call (800) 937-2628 or (708) 352-0606   (2006 prices)

• *Richardsons' Chartbook & Cruising Guide—Lake Erie Edition*
$89.99

· *Waterproof Chart #74 S. Lake Huron & Saginaw Bay*
$21.95

· *Waterproof Chart #75 N. Lake Huron & Straits of Mackinac*
$21.95

· *Richardsons' Lake Michigan Chartbook*
$69.95

· *Maptech Chart Kit: Florida West Coast and The Keys*
$129.95

· *Maptech Chart Kit: Norfolk to Jacksonville including ICW*
$129.95

· *Maptech Chart Kit: Chesapeake and Delaware Bays*
$129.95

The rest of the charts for the trip cover rivers, canals, and the New Jersey Coast. Many of the river charts are printed by the U.S. Army Corps of Engineers and can be ordered by writing to the district office in each region. A simple way of getting all the required charts is to order them from:

Marine Navigation, Inc.
613 S. LaGrange Road
LaGrange, IL 60525
Phone: (708) 352-0606 Fax: (708 352-2170)
e-mail: mnilaura@ameritech.net

Here are the charts you will need: Marine Navigation 2006 Prices

U.S. Army Corps of Engineers Charts:

· *Illinois Waterway Navigation Charts* $20.00
· *Upper Mississippi River Navigation Charts* $40.00

· *Ohio River Navigation Charts: Cairo IL to*
  Foster, KY $51.00

· *Cumberland River Charts* $17.00

The Barkley lock on the Cumberland River is less congested and usually a quicker lockage than the Kentucky lock on the Tennessee River.

· *Tennessee River Navigation Charts:*
  Paducah, KY to Pickwick, TN $28.00

· *Tombigbee Waterway*
  Pickwick, TN to Demopolis, AL $39.00

· *Lower Black Warrior River*
  Demopolis to Mobile, AL $36.00

NOAA Charts:

· *Mobile Bay to New Orleans, LA*
     11376 $19.25
     11378 $19.25
     11374 $19.25
     11372 $19.25
     11367 $19.25

· *Florida East Coast, ICW: Miami to Jacksonville*
     11467 $19.25
     11472 $19.25
     11485 $19.25
     11489 $19.25

· *Cape May, NJ to New York Harbor*
     12316 $19.25

12324	$19.25
12327	$19.25

- *New York State Canal System*

14786	$32.75

Embassy Waterproof Chart #4
   Hudson River: New York City to Troy Lock

Alternate Route Charts

NOAA Charts

- *Lake Champlain*

14781	$19.25
14782	$19.25
14783	$19.25
14784	$19.25
14785	$19.25

- *Riviere Richelieu*

Canadian Charts	Canadian Funds
1350	$28.00
1351	$28.00

- *St. Lawrence Seaway (Sorel, QUE to Kingston, ON)*

Canadian Charts	Canadian Funds
1311	$20.00
1310	$20.00
1409	$20.00
1431	$20.00
1432	$20.00
1433	$20.00
1434	$20.00
1435	$20.00

1436	$20.00
1437	$20.00
1438	$20.00
1439	$20.00

- *Ottawa River and Rideau River* (alternate to above)

Canadian Charts	Canadian Funds
1510	$18.00
1512	$23.00
1513	$33.00
1514	$18.00

> The "Erie Canal" is the longest of several canals on the N.Y.S.C.S. (Buffalo to Troy, NY). Others are Oswego Canal (Three Rivers to Oswego, NY), Cayuga-Seneca Canal (to Finger Lakes in New York), and Champlain Canal (continues north on Hudson River to Sorel on the St. Lawrence Seaway).

2.   GPS

I strongly recommend GPS over Loran since Loran signals are very weak in the northern part of Lake Huron and Lake Michigan. GPS is also much quicker and more accurate. I started the trip with a built-in Loran and a handheld GPS as a backup. I later converted the built-in Loran to a GPS; however, I still needed the handheld backup when the new GPS broke down six months later.

> Loran C is not going to be maintained in the future.

3.   Depth Finder

You need a good depth finder, especially in the intracoastal waterways and the Gulf of Mexico.

4.   Towing Insurance

We went from New Jersey to New Orleans without ever running aground. However, after running aground in Biloxi, Mississippi and then again on the West Coast of Florida Intracoastal, I bought unlimited towing insurance from Boat/US for $88.00 per year. We only ran aground one more time on the trip, but the insurance easily paid for itself.

5.   Radar

I strongly recommend radar. The very first day of our trip was all fog as we ran 98 miles off the New Jersey coast. We also encountered fog on the morning of our second and third days out. We later experienced fog several times on Lake Erie and on some of the rivers. Radar was also helpful in determining how far off shore we were in the Great Lakes on clear days. Lastly, radar assists you to run in the rain and can help avoid thunderstorms.

6.   VHS Radio with Cell Phone Backup

We used our VHS radio for NOAA marine forecasts every day and to communicate with other boats and mariners. However, there were times when a marina didn't answer on VHS but we were able to get them on the cell phone. Since almost the entire trip is in sight of land, the cell phone works everywhere. We kept the cell phone in the salon plugged into the battery charger and carried it to the bridge when under way.

7.   Autopilot

We did not have an autopilot, and we could not have used it very much if we had had one. The only places where you can use an autopilot are on the Great Lakes, while crossing the Gulf of Mexico, and while navigating the New Jersey coast. For the majority of the trip in rivers, canals, and Intracoastal waterways, your heading is constantly changing, which makes it difficult to use an autopilot system.

8.   Spare Props

We had spare props and needed them once; however, I understand from other boaters we met that we were lucky to only need them once. On a trip this long your chances of damaging a prop are pretty high, especially from floating debris.

9.   Shore Water and Two 50-Foot Lengths of Hose

We had our boat outfitted with a shore water connection, so when at dock we used fresh water. This way we did not deplete our onboard supply. Our boat has two heads and a stall shower, so we use lots of water. I found it a good idea to have two 50-foot hoses, one to connect to the onboard water system and one to wash the boat.

10.   Shore Power Y-Adapter (Two 30-Amp Inlets to One 50-Amp Inlet)

We have two 30-amp, 110-volt electric inlets and two 50-foot shore power cord sets. About 30 percent of the time we had to plug into a 50-amp outlet. The Y-adapter turned out to be very valuable.

11.   **Four-Step Stepladder**

We carried a four-step stepladder to help us get off the sides of our boat; this ladder folded flat for storage. With floating docks we could always get off the boat via a ladder to the swim platform. However, with fixed docks we often had to get off the boat from the side. Unfortunately, there could be up to four feet between our deck and the dock. We simply lowered the stepladder onto the fixed dock and stepped right off onto the ladder.

12.   **Cruising Guides**

In Chapter 3 I recommended that you purchase all the necessary cruising guides to help plan your trip; however, it is very important to bring them on the boat with you. You undoubtedly will go to some places on the trip that you didn't plan to, and you will need the cruising guides for that. Every single time you go to a marina you will need the individual chart blowups in the cruising guides, which show the location of each marina.

13.   **Handheld Halogen Light**

You will need a handheld halogen light with a ten-foot-long flexible cord that plugs into the cigarette lighter at the helm. This light will prove invaluable if it ever becomes absolutely *necessary* to run at night or to dock or anchor after dark. We started the trip without this light because we had a built-in searchlight. The searchlight turned out to be not nearly flexible or bright enough.

> **Not wise to run rivers in darkness. Do not take a chance and run at night. Stop early.**

14.   Navigation Tools

Besides a calculator and a set of parallel rules or a rolling plotter, I suggest a clipboard at the helm to hold a tablet with the day's navigation data listed. You will need good binoculars to read buoys and river mile markers. Lastly, I would suggest some large clips to put on the chart books at the helm to secure the pages.

15.   Fenders and Fender Adjusters

You will need at least six fenders to use when docking and in locks. In the N.Y.S.C.S. you will buy straw bags to use as fenders so the locks don't chew up your good fenders. By the time you have finished the N.Y.S.C.S. you will throw the straw bags away. We also recommend fender adjusters that allow you to raise and lower the fenders without untying the line.

16.   TV

TV reception on board can be good, bad, or nonexistent, depending on your situation. The best deal is an 18-inch satellite dish; however, this is fairly expensive. We had a TV aerial on the radar arch, that worked sometimes and not others. We also had a cable TV hookup on the boat. However, only about a third of the marinas we stayed at had cable service.

17.   Clothing

We experienced temperatures from the 50s to the 90s on the trip, although the great majority of the time we were able to wear shorts. We packed all of our clothes on board at the beginning of the trip and pretty much left them on board for the entire trip, even though we flew home three times. I only needed a coat and tie twice, once at the Grand Hotel in Mackinac Island and once at the Commodore Palace Restaurant in New Orleans (both recommended). Laundry was not a problem, since most of the marinas we stayed at had facilities.

18. Food and Supplies

We stocked the boat with food, drink, cleaning supplies, etc. at the beginning of the trip and replenished weekly as we traveled. Marina ship stores have a few items, but usually we went to a supermarket every week. Often the marina would have a courtesy car we could borrow to go shopping. If we were staying at a place for a while, we often rented a car for a few days (Enterprise Rent a Car will pick you up at the marina).

> **Holding tanks are required in the Great Lakes and inland waters. Check CFR and/or state laws.**

THE TRIP

Avalon, NJ to Buffalo, NY

Hudson River and Erie Canal

CHAPTER 5

AVALON TO BUFFALO
HUDSON RIVER AND ERIE CANAL

DESTINATION	MARINA	STATUTE MILES	CUMULATIVE MILES
(Depart Avalon, NJ)	(Home Port)	0	
Atlantic City, NJ	Harrah's Casino		
Manasquan Inlet, NJ	Brielle Yacht Club	96	96
New York City, NY			
Tarrytown, NY	Tarrytown Marina	63	159
Kingston, NY			
Troy, NY	Troy Town Dock	109	268
Fultonville, NY	Poplars Inn & Marina	48	316
Rome, NY	Riverside Marina	66	382
Baldwinsville, NY	Coopers Marina	58	440
Fairport, NY	Town Dock	74	514
Lockport, NY	Goehle Municipal	74	588
Buffalo, NY	Erie Basin Marina	34	622

Charts Required: *NOAA Chart 12327*
Embassy #4—Hudson River Chart
14786—New York State Canal System

Cruising Guide: *Waterway Guide—Northern*

(On the preceding page, the destinations where the author stayed are shown in bold type. These destinations are described in the following chapter. The other destinations are listed as intermediate ports if a shorter cruising day is desired. Check the cruising guide for information on intermediate ports.)

Cape May to Atlantic City

The trip from Cape May to Atlantic City is 41 statute miles. The simplest way to make this trip is in the ocean running about 2 miles off of the beach. There is an Intracoastal Waterway in New Jersey; however, it has some problems. The inland waterway is very shallow in the Wildwood area, and there are so many bridges in the Atlantic City area that have to open, it is usually much easier to go outside.

Enter the inlet and about 1.5 miles in you will see the Frank Farley State Marina on the left; a little farther is the Harrah's Casino Marina. The Frank Farley State Marina is next to the Trump Castle Casino. Therefore, the marina that you stay at depends on your Casino choice. We stayed at Harrah's.

> **The ICW is subject to change. Get latest information and local knowledge.**

Atlantic City

Atlantic City has had a rebirth with the coming of all the casinos. Compared to Las Vegas, there are not very many casinos in Atlantic City, only 14; however, they are very large. Even if you don't gamble, the casino marinas are a great place to stay because they offer many restaurants and lots of entertainment at reasonable prices. The cheapest hotel room in Harrah's Casino Hotel is probably $200, however, we paid only $35 for a 40-foot boat slip and you can order room service on your boat.

Harrah's Casino Marina
    Phone: (609) 441-5315

Approach Depth	25'	Diesel Fuel	no
Dockside Depth	15'	Mechanical Repairs	no
Accepts Transients	yes	Ships Store	no
Dockside Power	30,50	Showers	yes
Dockside Water	yes	Laundromat	yes
Gasoline	no	Restaurant	yes

Atlantic City to Brielle, New Jersey

The trip from Atlantic City to Brielle, New Jersey at the Manasquan Inlet, is 57 statute miles running on the outside and about 70 miles on the inside. The inside route includes the Barnegat Bay and there are a lot of no-wake areas. If the weather is nice, I recommend the outside route running several miles off of the beach. Using the NOAA charts 12316 and 12324, cruise up the coast to Manasquan Inlet.

> **Get latest information on conditions.**

Go into the Manasquan Inlet and the marinas are about 1 mile in. We stayed at the Brielle Yacht Club, which has a nice facility. There are several restaurants right there.

Brielle Yacht Club Marina
    201 Union Lane
    Brielle, NJ 08730
    Phone: (908) 528-6250

Approach Depth	12'	Diesel Fuel	yes
Dockside Depth	12'	Mechanical Repairs	no
Accepts Transients	yes	Ships Store	yes
Dockside Power	30,50	Showers	yes
Dockside Water	yes	Laundromat	no
Gasoline	yes	Restaurant	yes

Brielle, New Jersey to New York City

The trip from Brielle to New York City is 44 statute miles. The New Jersey ICW ends at the northern end of Barnegat Bay, south of the Manasquan Inlet. Therefore, the trip from Brielle to New York City must be in the ocean.

Using NOAA charts 12324 and 12327, cruise along the shore to Sandy Hook. Several miles north of Sandy Hook is the Ambrose Channel, the main ship channel into New York Harbor. Follow the Ambrose Channel under the Verrazano Bridge into New York Harbor.

The Hudson River

The part of the Hudson that is on our trip goes from New York City to Troy, New York, beginning with the New York Harbor, which is one of the most spectacular sites on the entire trip. Cruising up to the Statue of Liberty in your own boat is quite the thrill. This is obviously a photo-op to get everyone on deck for a photograph with the Statue of Liberty in the background. The Battery is also a spectacular view from the water. In fact, the entire cruise up the Hudson alongside New York City is exciting. As you cruise north, you pass one landmark after another, such as the George Washington Bridge, the Palisades, Yonkers, Tappan Zee Bridge, Bear Mountain Bridge, West Point, Newburgh, N.Y., Poughkeepsie, N.Y., Hyde Park (Roosevelt's home), Kingston, N.Y., Albany, N.Y., and Troy, N.Y.

The Hudson River has a current, which can be several knots, and after a rainstorm, floating debris can be a problem. For most of the way, from the Tappan Zee Bridge to Troy, the view is of beautiful rolling hills with large estates and farms coming down to the water. As you approach Albany from the south, with farms on either side of the river, the skyscrapers of the New York State Capital suddenly appear as you round a bend. A trip up the Hudson is worthwhile.

New York City

New York City is a great place to spend several days of sightseeing. You can visit the United Nations, Broadway theaters, Lincoln Center, the New York Stock Exchange, museums, great restaurants and much, much more. To have access to everything in Manhattan, one of the best marinas to stay in is the Newport Marina, located on the New Jersey side of the Hudson but only a 5-minute walk to the subway train to Manhattan. All the marinas with transient slips are on the New Jersey side of the Hudson.

Newport Marina
    500 Washington Blvd.
    Jersey City, NJ 07310
    (201) 626-5552
    www.newportnj.com

Approach Depth	14'	Diesel Fuel	no
Dockside Depth	23'	Mechanical Repairs	yes
Accepts Transients	yes	Ships Store	yes
Dockside Power	30,50,100	Showers	yes
Dockside Water	yes	Laundromat	yes
Gasoline	no	Restaurant	yes

New York City to Tarrytown, N.Y.

The Hudson River Channel is well marked and the channel is deep, varying from 15 feet to 175 feet deep. Since there had been a large rainstorm during the week, we ran into a substantial current and had to dodge some floating debris. We had sunshine and enjoyed the beautiful scenery all the way. Immediately after passing under the Tappan Zee Bridge, you turn right into the Tarrytown Marina.

Tarrytown, N.Y

Tarrytown, New York was made famous by Washington Irving's *The Legend of Sleepy Hollow*. Washington Irving's house, outside of town, is open to the public.

Tarrytown Marina
236 W. Main Street
Tarrytown, NY 10591
(914) 631-1300
www.tarrytownboatclub.com

Approach Depth	15'	Diesel Fuel	yes
Dockside Depth	15'	Mechanical Repairs	yes
Accepts Transients	yes	Ships Store	yes
Dockside Power	yes	Showers	yes

| Dockside Water | yes | Laundromat | yes |
| Gasoline | yes | Restaurant | yes |

Tarrytown to Troy, N.Y.

We started our trip from Tarrytown to Troy in dense fog. We used the radar to keep in the middle of the river. The fog lifted just in time for us to see West Point, which is very imposing from the water; it looks like a massive fort built on cliffs on the west side of the river. We continued to see floating debris, a result of strong rainstorms during the last few days. Also, partially as a result of the rainstorms, we were bucking a 3-mph current. It took 7.5 hours to do 109 miles from Tarrytown to Troy, an average of 14 mph, though we were cruising around 17 mph. We enjoyed the beautiful scenery and were amazed at how little traffic was on this large river.

Troy, New York

We stayed at Troy Town Dock, a 1,000-foot-long floating dock in front of a 20-foot-high stone wall in downtown Troy. From the dock you walk up 20 feet of stairs to get to street level. The marina office is at street level, where you buy straw bags for the N.Y.S.C.S. Straw bags are disposable fenders; by the time you have made it to Buffalo they are thrown away. We had a 40-foot boat, so we bought 6 bags at $5.00 each and put them all on the starboard side. As it turned out, we were able to dock on the starboard side all but two times. Twice, because of repairs on the lock, we were directed to dock on our port side. When this occurred, we used our permanent fenders instead of moving the straw bags.

Across the street from the marina office is a microbrewery with a restaurant. We tried all six kinds of beer.

Troy Town Dock Marina
    427 River Street #2
    Troy, NY 12180
    (518) 272-5341
    www.troytowndock.com

Approach Depth	16'	Diesel Fuel	yes
Dockside Depth	21'	Mechanical Repairs	yes
Accepts Transients	yes	Ships Store	yes
Dockside Power	30,50	Showers	yes
Dockside Water	yes	Laundromat	yes
Gasoline	yes	Restaurant	yes

The N.Y.S.C.S. (the Erie Canal)

The N.Y.S.C.S. was the first important waterway built in the United States. The canal runs from Buffalo on Lake Erie across New York State to Troy and Albany on the Hudson so traffic can then go down the Hudson to New York City. By connecting the Great Lakes with the Atlantic Ocean the canal provides a route for manufactured goods to flow west and raw materials to flow east.

The canal was opened in 1825; at that time New York City was second to Philadelphia in population and as a port. Ten years after the canal opened, the Port of New York was larger than the Port of Philadelphia. Twenty years after the canal opened, the city of New York had become the largest city in the United States.

The original canal was 363 miles long. It was 28 feet wide at the bottom, 42 feet wide at the top, and 4 feet deep. It could carry boats that were 80 feet long and 15 feet wide with a draft of 3.5 feet. By 1862 the canal had been enlarged several times. The present-day N.Y.S.C.S. was constructed near the old canal and opened in 1918.

Today the canal has a depth of 10 feet and all locks are 44.5 feet wide and 300 feet long. Even though it is called the New York State Barge Canal System, there are very few barges on the canal. The overwhelming majority of boat traffic is recreational.

There are two routes to take on the N.Y.S.C.S., depending on your boat's height above the waterline. If your boat is 15.5 feet or less, you can take the canal from Troy to Buffalo. If your boat is between 15.5 feet and 19 feet, you can take the canal to Oswego, N.Y. on Lake Ontario, then take Lake Ontario to the Welland Canal, and the Welland Canal to Buffalo.

> The author's boat measured 15.75 and he should have travelled to Oswego, Lake Ontario, and the Welland Canal.

> Vertical clearance is incorrectly stated. NOAA Chart 14786, New York State Canal System, states:
>
> VERTICAL CLEARANCE: Minimum vertical clearance at Maximum Navigable Pool Level under bridges and gates, along:
>   A. Champlain, Cayuga & Seneca Canal and the Erie Canal west of Three Rivers . . . 15.5 feet
>   B. Oswego Canal and the Erie Canal east of Three Rivers . . . 20 feet.

If you take the canal to Oswego on Lake Ontario, you will travel 180 miles and traverse 31 locks, rising to 420 feet elevation at Rome, N.Y. and descending to 246 feet on Lake Ontario. If you take the canal to Buffalo, you will travel 363 miles and traverse 36 locks, rising to 572 feet on Lake Erie.

The speed limit on the entire length of the canal is 10 mph, except on Lake Oneida. Each lock takes about 25 minutes, so plan on four days to Oswego and six days to Buffalo. The cost was $15 per day; however, they had two-day tickets for $20, so we bought three tickets for $60.

We took the canal to Buffalo, but we had to take our radome down to get to 15.75 feet. Despite this precaution, we actually scraped on the lowest bridge.

Passing through a lock is an interesting experience. When approaching, you must stop at a safe distance and wait for the gates to open and a green light before proceeding. If you have questions, you can talk to the lockmaster on channel 10 on your VHF radio. Once the green light comes on, you proceed slowly (4 mph) into the lock and dock against the side of the lock. Approximately every 30 feet the lock will have lines that are connected at the top and hang over the side. Depending on the size of your boat, a crew member grabs hold of this line to hold the boat close to the wall of the lock. Since our boat was 40 feet long, we needed to hang onto two lines. These lines are very dirty, and you will need leather work gloves to handle them. After you have finished the canal, you will throw these gloves away (or frame them!).

Locks can easily handle ten or more pleasure boats at a time. However, usually you are in the lock by yourself or with two or three other boats. Since the speed limit is 10 mph, the lockmasters expect that if there are three boats in lock 4 they will all arrive at lock 5 together. The lockmasters call ahead to the next lock to say that three boats have passed lock 4 so the next lock can be ready with the water at the correct level and the gates open when the three boats arrive. If one of those boats decides to speed at 20 mph, the lockmaster at the next lock will make the fast boat wait at the lock until the boats traveling at the speed limit are safely in the lock.

Most of the locks are raising your boat; however, on the Buffalo route there are three lowering locks, and on the Oswego route there are eleven lowering locks. Locks that raise your boat are easier, because you come into the lock at the lowest level and you are protected from the wind. The wind can be a problem in locks that lower your boat, since you come into the lock with most of your boat above the lock walls.

The N.Y.S.C.S. locks range from 6 feet to 40.5 feet in vertical lift. All the locks work by gravity, with the lockmaster operating hydraulic valves to either raise or lower the water level in the lock.

Several weeks before you plan to go onto the N.Y.S.C.S. it is a good idea to call the Canal System at (518) 471-5011 to make sure the canal is fully operational. The canal is generally closed from sometime in October to sometime in May because of ice. However, parts of the canal can also close for a period in spring and summer because of high water levels or other problems.

Troy to Fultonville

Lock No. 1 is at Troy on the Hudson River, so the canal actually starts with Lock 2. Locks 2 through 6 are all quite close together; however, combined they lift your boat 170 feet. Lock No. 8 is in Schenectady, N.Y.

We stopped for the night at Fultonville, N.Y., a few miles beyond Lock No. 12 and 48 miles from Lock No. 2. We stayed at Poplars Inn and Marina, a motel with a restaurant and swimming pool. The floating dock on the side of the canal, with no electricity or water, is the only place to stay on this part of the canal. We used our generator to provide electricity. We had dinner at their restaurant and used the pool.

Fulton to Rome

The second day on the N.Y.S.C.S. includes 66 miles and 8 locks. Lock

17, with a 40.5 foot lift, is highest on the N.Y.S.C.S. and higher than any of the Panama Canal locks.

The scenery all along the canal is rural, with farms, fields, and woods.   The N.Y.S.C.S. locks are beautifully maintained—freshly painted and most sporting flower gardens. At 10 mph in this pastoral setting, you think you have gone back in time.

Utica, N.Y. is between Locks 19 and 20. Our destination for the night was the Riverside Marina in Rome, N.Y., about 10 miles beyond Utica at an elevation of 420 feet. You cannot see this marina from the canal; a sign with an arrow directs you to turn left into what looks like a creek and go under a stone bridge.   Then you see the marina.

In Rome there is an excellent restaurant called the Savoy. They will pick you up for dinner and return you to the marina.

Riverside Marina
6805 Martin Street
Rome, NY 13440
(315) 337-5199

Approach Depth	5'	Diesel Fuel	no
Dockside Depth	6'	Mechanical Repairs	yes
Accepts Transients	yes	Ships Store	no
Dockside Power	30,50	Showers	no
Dockside Water	yes	Laundromat	no
Gasoline	yes	Restaurant	no

Rome to Baldwinsville, NY

From Rome to Baldwinsville is 58 miles.

After Rome you go through Locks 21 and 22 that lower your boat 50 feet to the level of Lake Oneida. Prior to these two locks, all the locks have been raising your boat.

Lake Oneida is about 22 miles long; you follow channel markers across. There is no speed limit on this lake. There are marinas with fuel on either end of the lake.

After the lake you encounter Lock 23 and then Three Rivers where the Oswego Canal joins the N.Y.S.C.S. If you are taking the Lake Ontario route to Buffalo, you leave the N.Y.S.C.S. here and take the Oswego Canal north.

> **The Oswego Canal to Lake Ontario, then to the Welland Canal to Port Colborne and continue from there westward.**

If you are going to Buffalo all the way on the N.Y.S.C.S., you turn left at Three Rivers.

After Three Rivers, the next lock is Lock 24; the next town is Baldwinsville, N.Y., a suburb of Syracuse. We stayed at Cooper's Marina, on the canal.

Cooper's Marina
2302 W. Genesee Road
Baldwinsville, NY 13027
(315) 635-7371
www.coopersmarina.com

Approach Depth	10'	Diesel Fuel	yes
Dockside Depth	10'	Mechanical Repairs	yes
Accepts Transients	yes	Ships Store	yes
Dockside Power	yes	Showers	yes
Dockside Water	yes	Laundromat	yes
Gasoline	yes	Restaurant	across street

Baldwinsville to Fairport

From Baldwinsville to Fairport is 74 miles and 7 locks. The lowest bridge, with less than 16-feet clearance, is in this section. We got down to 15.75 feet by removing our radome, but we scraped the bridge.

> **At 15.75 feet, the boat should have exited at Three Rivers and transited the Welland Canal to Port Colborne.**

About 30 miles from Baldwinsville the Cayuga-Seneca Canal connects with the N.Y.S.C.S. If you wish to visit the Finger Lakes as a side trip, you take this canal.

Fairport is between Lock 30 and Lock 32—there is no Lock 31. Fairport is a pretty town, with a lift bridge and brick sidewalks on either side of the canal. There is no marina here and no fuel; however, their canal frontage is the nicest on the entire canal. We paid $7 for a 50-amp electric hookup and a water hookup for the night. There are several restaurants within short walking distance.

Fairport to Lockport, N.Y.

Fairport to Lockport is 74 miles and 2 locks. After going through Locks 32 and 33, the canal runs through the city of Rochester, N.Y. From Rochester to Lockport is more than 50 miles without any locks.

We stayed at the Goehle Municipal Marina, a park with a docking facility. They had 20-amp electric service; we require 50 amps, so we had to run our generator. We took a cab into town for dinner, which was unusual since the great majority of the time either a nice restaurant was within walking distance, or else the marina or restaurant provided a courtesy car.

Lockport to Buffalo, N.Y.

From Lockport to Buffalo the distance is 34 miles; the last 9 miles are on the Niagara River.

Locks 34 and 35 are in Lockport and are a "flight"; when you come out of Lock 34 you go right into Lock 35. These locks end the actual canal; from here to the Niagara River you are on the Tonawanda River.

Buffalo Harbor has a three-mile-long breakwater that protects the harbor from lake waves. You enter the breakwater at the northern end when coming from the Niagara River and then into the Black Rock lock and canal that bypasses the strong currents in the Niagara River. The canal has a 6-mph speed limit. At the end of the canal is the Erie Basin Marina, an excellent, large marina surrounded by high-rise condos with water views.

Erie Basin Marina
329 Erie Street
Buffalo, NY 14202
(716) 851-5389

Approach Depth	29'	**Diesel Fuel**	yes
Dockside Depth	23'	**Mechanical Repairs**	yes
Accepts Transients	yes	**Ships Store**	yes
Dockside Power	30,50,100	**Showers**	yes
Dockside Water	yes	**Laundromat**	no
Gasoline	yes	**Restaurant**	short walk

The trip begins
Crew #1: Bob Lande, Bick Remmey and Buzz Mead

The Statue of Liberty

New York Harbor

An Erie Canal lock—locking up

BUFFALO TO DETROIT

LAKE ERIE

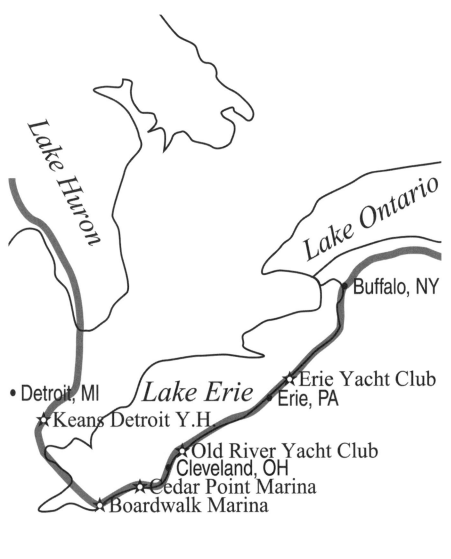

Lake Huron

Lake Ontario

• Buffalo, NY

• Detroit, MI *Lake Erie* ☆Erie Yacht Club
Erie, PA
☆Keans Detroit Y.H.

☆Old River Yacht Club
Cleveland, OH
☆Cedar Point Marina
☆Boardwalk Marina

OHIO

CHAPTER 6

BUFFALO TO DETROIT
LAKE ERIE

DESTINATION	MARINA	STATUTE MILES	CUMULATIVE MILES
(Depart Buffalo, NY)			
Dunkirk, NY			
Erie, PA	Erie Yacht Club	82	704
Ashtabula, OH			
Cleveland, OH	Olde River Yacht Club	101	805
Sandusky, OH	Cedar Point Marina	64	869
Put-in-Bay, OH	Boardwalk Marina	21	890
Detroit, MI	Keans Detroit Yacht Harbor	52	942

Charts Required:
   Richardsons' Chart Book and Cruising Guide—Lake Erie

Cruising Guide:
   Lakeland Boating Ports O'Call Lakes Erie & St. Clair

(On the preceding page, the destinations where the author stayed are shown in bold type. These destinations are described in the following chapter. The other destinations are listed as intermediate ports if a shorter cruising day is desired. Check *Ports O'Call* for information on intermediate ports.)

Lake Erie

The tour of the "Rust Belt" from the water turned out to be much nicer than expected. Most marine facilities were very good and the skylines of Cleveland and Detroit are spectacular from the water. The marinas where we stayed in Buffalo, Erie, and Cleveland were particularly nice, all with good restaurants on location. The resort areas of Cedar Point and Put-In-Bay were well worth the visit, independent of the boat trip.

Lake Erie, the fourth largest of the Great Lakes, is 241 miles long and 56 miles wide at its widest point. Its average depth is only 56 feet, which accounts for the choppy water that can build quickly with an increase in wind speed. Because of the lake's position, it is subject to sudden afternoon squalls and thunderstorms. Consequently, I recommend that you plan to arrive at your destination by 3 P.M., which will beat most of the bad weather.

Lake Erie has some problems that you may or may not encounter: fog and floating debris. We encountered both. We had some dense fog on several days, and without radar, we could not have moved. Lake Erie is fed by many rivers and streams, and after a period of rainstorms, particularly thunderstorms, tree branches and other floating debris are carried into the lake. We were on Lake Erie after several strong thunderstorms had passed, so we saw a lot of floating debris for several days.

On the trip from Buffalo to Cedar Point I recommend that you cruise one to two miles off shore, because the water is deep and there is no reason to go out any farther into the lake. Also, Lake Erie is heavily traveled by commercial shipping that you will rarely see when traveling close to shore.

From Cedar Point to Put-In-Bay and from there to the Detroit River you are cruising across the lake, so you must navigate by compass and GPS.

Our trip followed the southern shore, which starts out in New York and then follows the Pennsylvania shore and the Ohio shore to Cedar Point. The southern shore of the lake has interesting destinations; the northern shore, which is Ontario, Canada, has no major cities, only small fishing villages.

Buffalo

Sights to see in Buffalo include the Allentown Historic District of beautiful nineteenth-century mansions, one of which is the Theodore Roosevelt National Historic Site. Other attractions include the art and historical museums plus a naval museum with several World War II naval ships. Buffalo invented Buffalo Wings, so be sure to try these spicy chicken wings at the local restaurants.

Niagara Falls, an hour's drive from the marina area, is worth a visit. The couple who did the Lake Erie part of our trip with us had never been to Niagara Falls, so we rented a car for the day and went to the falls. It definitely qualifies as one of the natural wonders of the world.

Buffalo is one of the places where you might consider renting a car, not only for sightseeing, but also to get to the restaurants in the downtown area. Crawdaddy's is a large restaurant next to the Erie Basin Marina. We went there twice because of good food and a great view.

Buffalo to Erie, Pennsylvania
Richardsons' Chart Book—Lake Erie Edition

Our navigation plan was to follow the shoreline about two miles off from Buffalo to Erie. One of the nice things about cruising the Great Lakes is that you don't normally have to worry about running aground.

We made the 82-mile trip from Buffalo to Erie in 4 hours and 48 minutes. We left in a steady rain and had to dodge a lot of floating logs in the lake. By the time we got to the Erie Yacht Club it was sunny.

Erie, Pennsylvania

The entrance to the Erie City port is on the east end of the Presque Isle Peninsula. This peninsula connects to the mainland at its western end and is open at its eastern end. The peninsula creates the Presque Isle Bay, which is 4.5 miles long and .5 miles wide.

The city is on the southern shore of the bay, while the northern shore is a State Park. The park has a marina about a mile and a half west of the harbor entrance. This marina has no specific transient docks; however, the dockmaster can usually find you a slip left open by one of the resident boats.

No public transportation is available from the park to the city, but there are several restaurants in the dock area and some of Erie's most interesting sights are within walking distance.

We stayed at the Erie Yacht Club, several miles south from downtown on the bay. To stay at the Erie Yacht Club, you must be a member of another yacht club and also make a reservation. Erie Yacht Club has excellent facilities and a first-class restaurant. The restaurant is closed on Monday.

Erie Yacht Club

1 Ravine Drive
Erie, PA 16505
(814) 453-4931 Office
(814) 456-9914 Gas Dock
www.erieyachtclub.com

Approach Depth	N/A	Diesel Fuel	Yes
Dockside Depth	Floating docks	Mechanical Repairs	No
Accepts Transients	Yes	Ships Store	No
Dockside Power	110	Showers	Yes
Dockside Water	Yes	Laundromat	No
Gasoline	Yes	Restaurant	Yes

Erie to Cleveland
Richardsons' Chart Book—Lake Erie Edition

As with the previous day, our plan was to cruise two miles off shore to Cleveland. We planned to make the 111-mile trip from Erie to Cleveland in one day, but the threat of early afternoon thunderstorms caused us to make a stop in Fairport, 24 miles short of Cleveland. We left Erie in sunshine, but we were rained on six different times that day, the last three after we had arrived in Fairport.

We had an interesting experience with our radar. We saw what looked like one large rainstorm up ahead, but the radar showed it was two distinct squalls. We set our course to go between the two and only experienced a few minutes of rain.

The next morning we tried to leave Fairport at 9:00 A.M. but had to turn back because of dense fog. At 11:00 A.M. we followed a fishing boat out of the harbor into the lake, where visibility was about one-half mile. Visibility was one mile by the time we got to Cleveland.

Cleveland

Cleveland, Ohio is 111 miles down the coast from Erie, Pennsylvania and 63 miles from Ashtabula, Ohio. Cleveland is a major city making a strong comeback; a lot of its improvements are on the waterfront.

The city waterfront is protected by a 5-mile long breakwater that creates a harbor. There are three entrances: one at the far northeast end, the main entrance at the Cuyahoga River, and the entrance at the far southeast end. We took the main entrance.

Immediately after passing underneath the railroad lift bridge, turn to starboard into Old River and go approximately one mile to the Old River Yacht Club, which is on the right. The Old River Yacht Club is a new facility with a very nice restaurant and swimming pool.

If you are going to stay in Cleveland for a few days, I recommend you rent a car, because there is so much to see and do. Along the Cuyahoga River are many nightclubs and restaurants. In downtown Cleveland, near the stadium where the Cleveland Indians play, is the Rock and Roll Hall of Fame. When we visited, we were surprised to find that this is really a museum of American music, including Dixieland and Country music as well as Rock and Roll. On Euclid Avenue is the Old Arcade, a nineteenth-century enclosed mall of structural iron and glass, where elegant shops surround a central atrium on five balcony levels. A little farther along Euclid is Cleveland's restored theater district, known as Playhouse Square.

Olde River Yacht Club
　　4900 Whiskey Island
　　Cleveland, OH 44102
　　(216) 631-9100
　　www.olderiveryachtclub.com

Approach Depth	10'	Diesel Fuel		no
Dockside Depth (min)	6.6'	Mechanical Repairs		no
Accepts Transients	yes	Ships Store		no
Dockside Power	30,50	Showers		yes
Dockside Water	yes	Laundromat		yes
Gasoline	no	Restaurant		yes
VHF channels 17,68				

Cleveland to Cedar Point, Sandusky Bay, Ohio
Richardsons' Chart Book—Lake Erie Edition

We continued to cruise about two miles off shore from Cleveland to Cedar Point. Our trip from Cleveland to Cedar Point was bumpy because our course was west and the winds were from the west at 15 knots. It was a sunny day, and we made the 64-mile trip in a little over four hours.

Cedar Point

Next to Sandusky, Ohio is a peninsula that protrudes about one mile into the lake, with the Cedar Point Amusement Park on the end. Follow the Mosely Channel around the tip of Cedar Point to get to the Cedar Point Marina. The amusement park gate is next to the marina, and there is free bus service for the Cedar Point complex.

Cedar Point is the roller coaster capital of the world, with six roller coasters. The Cedar Point roller coasters are some of the scariest anywhere. One of them has 4 people across, standing up—clamped in. This roller coaster does a 360° loop; the people are upside down at the top of the loop.

Besides the amusement park, the complex includes two hotels, a sandy beach, and several restaurants.

Cedar Point Marina
1 Cedar Point Drive
Sandusky, OH 44870
(888) 273-6257
www.cedarpoint.com

Approach Depth	10'	Diesel Fuel	yes
Dockside Depth	8'	Mechanical Repairs	yes
Accepts Transients	yes	Ships Store	yes
Dockside Power	30,50	Showers	yes
Dockside Water	yes	Laundromat	yes
Gasoline	yes	Restaurant	yes

Cedar Point to Put-In-Bay
Richardsons' Chart Book—Lake Erie Edition

We originally had planned to go to Pelee Island, Canada from Cedar Point, only 38 miles away but due north. The wind that day had shifted and was blowing from the north, creating 4- to 5-foot waves. Because of the wind direction, we decided to go west to Put-In-Bay. This turned out to be a good decision, not only because we had a smooth ride, but also because Put-In-Bay is a great place.

Using *Richardsons' Chart Book—Lake Erie Edition,* the 21-mile trip from Cedar Point to Put-In-Bay is as follows: Take the Moseley Channel to the end and then turn due north to the center of the south passage. Go west, passing just south of south Bass Island. Follow the west coast of South Bass Island to Put-In-Bay.

Put-In-Bay

Put-In-Bay is the only town on South Bass Island. The entire island is recreational, and a great way to see it is to rent a bicycle, moped, or golf cart. A must-see is the Perry Monument, where park rangers tell the story of Perry's famous victory in the 1813 Battle of Lake Erie. The view from the top of the monument is spectacular on a clear day: you can see the tall buildings of Detroit and Cleveland.

We rented a golf cart that held four people, two sitting forward and two sitting backward. We toured the entire island, which is very picturesque. Bill Gardner and my wife Jeri took a 12-minute plane ride in a replica of a 1935 biplane with open cockpits. We had a fresh seafood dinner that night at the restaurant on the dock at the Boardwalk Marina and listened to the music of Eddie Boggs Band.

Boardwalk Marina
> 1 Bayview Avenue
> Put-In-Bay, OH 43456
> Phone: (419) 285-6183

Approach Depth	8'	Diesel Fuel	no
Dockside Depth	8'	Mechanical Repairs	yes
Accepts Transients	yes	Ships Store	no
Dockside Power	30	Showers	no
Dockside Water	yes	Laundromat	no
Gasoline	yes	Restaurant	yes

Put-In-Bay to Detroit, Michigan
Richardsons' Chart Book—Lake Erie Edition

Our trip from Put-In-Bay to Detroit was on a beautiful sunny day with smooth seas. We left at 8:45 A.M. and arrived at 12:30 P.M.

From Put-In-Bay to the marinas north of downtown Detroit is 52 miles. When leaving Put-In-Bay, cruise past Rattlesnake Island and then set a northwest course for the Detroit River Channel.

We stayed at Keans Detroit Yacht Harbor, a large marina with 400 slips and a large service department capable of every type of marine repair. We needed some repairs, so we were glad to be there.

Detroit, Michigan

If you plan to spend time in Detroit, I recommend a rental car. Enterprise Car Rental will pick you up at the marina and take you to their offices to pick up your car. Places to see in Detroit include Greek Town, Renaissance Center, and The Henry Ford Museum. Detroit also has some excellent museums and restaurants. While you're in the area, you may wish to take a side trip to visit Greenfield Village in Dearborn, Michigan.

We stayed a total of four days in Detroit. We arrived on a Monday and went to Greek Town for dinner that night. Tuesday we went sightseeing at The Henry Ford Museum and Greenfield Village, which is a collection of the actual homes and workplaces of famous inventors—Henry Ford's birthplace and the original Ford Motor Company building, Thomas Edison's Menlo Park Laboratory, and the Wright Brothers' home and bicycle shop. Wednesday we drove Ann and Bill Gardner to the Detroit Airport for their flight back to Philadelphia. Thursday we picked up our next crew, Jim and Nancy Hoffman, who were flying in from Colorado. Repairs were completed on Thursday, and we were ready to start the next leg of our trip on Friday.

Keans Detroit Yacht Harbor
    100 Meadowbrook Street
    Detroit, MI 48214-0189
    (313) 822-4500
    www.marinas.com/keansdetroityachtharbor/

Approach Depth	8'	Diesel Fuel	no
Dockside Depth	7'	Mechanical Repairs	yes
Accepts Transients	yes	Ships Store	yes
Dockside Power	30	Showers	yes
Dockside Water	yes	Laundromat	yes
Gasoline	yes	Restaurant	no

Nittany Navy at the Erie, Pennsylvania Yacht Club

Harbor at Put-In-Bay

Renaissance Center in Detroit

DETROIT TO MACKINAC ISLAND

LAKE HURON

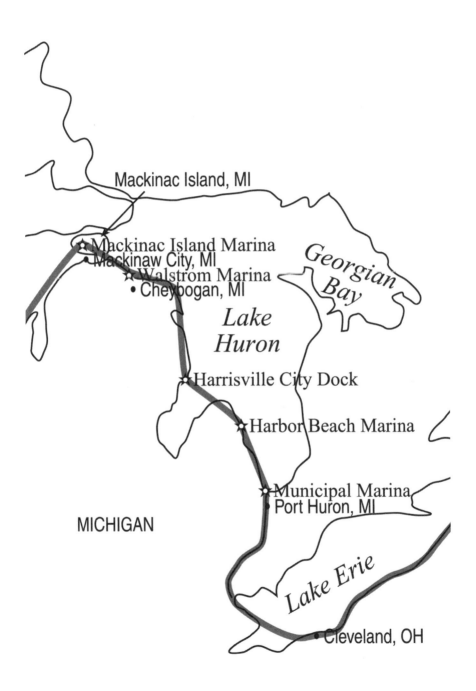

CHAPTER 7

DETROIT TO MACKINAC ISLAND
LAKE HURON

DESTINATION	MARINA	STATUTE MILES	CUMULATIVE MILES
(Depart Detroit)			
Port Huron, MI	Municipal Marina	50	992
Harbor Beach, MI	Harbor Beach Marina	55	1047
Harrisville, MI	Harrisville City Dock	55	1102
Rogers City, MI			
Cheboygan, MI	Walstrom Marina	91	1193
Mackinac Island, MI	Mackinac Island Marina	14	1207

Charts Required:
> *Richardsons' Chart Book and Cruising Guide—Lake Erie*
> *Chart #74 S. Lake Huron & Saginaw Bay*
> *Chart #75 N. Lake Huron & Straits of Mackinac*

Cruising Guide:
> *Lakeland Boating Ports O'Call Lake Huron*

(On the preceding page, the destinations where the author stayed are shown in bold type. These destinations are described in the following chapter. The other destinations are listed as intermediate ports if a shorter cruising day is desired. Check the cruising guide for information on intermediate ports.)

Detroit to Port Huron
Richardsons' Chart Book and Cruising Guide—Lake Erie Edition

We left Detroit at 9 A.M. and arrived at Port Huron at 12:15 P.M. You follow the Detroit River to Lake St. Clair. After crossing the lake following the clearly marked channel, you enter the St. Clair River. The St. Clair River takes you to Port Huron, the entrance to Lake Huron. We had a beautiful, sunny day and the ride was smooth. We stayed at the municipal marina in Port Huron.

Port Huron

In addition to the Municipal Marina, Port Huron has several private marinas and a yacht club, all on the Black River. Restaurants and shopping are within walking distance from the Municipal Marina. We had an excellent dinner at the Edison Inn, which was not in walking distance; however, they sent a courtesy car to take us to and from the restaurant. Sarinia, Canada is located across the St. Clair River from Port Huron. Sarinia is an industrial city much larger than Port Huron. If you would prefer to stay in Canada, Sarinia has good marina facilities; however, you must clear Customs.

Port Huron Municipal Marina
2021 Water Street
Port Huron, MI 48060
Phone: (810) 984-9745

Approach Depth	28'	Diesel Fuel	yes
Dockside Depth	15'	Mechanical Repairs	no
Accepts Transients	yes	Ships Store	no
Dockside Power	30,50	Showers	yes
Dockside Water	yes	Laundromat	yes
Gasoline	yes	Restaurant	yes

Lake Huron

Lake Huron is the second largest of the Great Lakes. It is different from the other lakes in that there are no large cities on Lake Huron. The character of the lake is very rural, with all ports being small towns or villages. Since our route followed the Michigan shore, we usually were within several miles of shore except when crossing Saginaw Bay. The lake is deep; even though we were close to shore, we were usually running in 40 feet of water or more. As you travel north, the temperature drops— the temperature in Mackinac Island is significantly cooler than Port Huron. We spent the Fourth of July on Mackinac Island and needed a sweater in the morning and evening. We found the Loran signals to be very weak in the northern part of the lake; however, the GPS signals were strong.

Port Huron to Harbor Beach
Chart #74 S. Lake Huron & Saginaw Bay

It took us 3.5 hours to travel the 55 miles from Port Huron to Harbor Beach, running along the Michigan shoreline. It was a sunny day but windy. A storm was predicted to hit our area in midafternoon, so we left at 8:00 A.M. and arrived at 11:30 A.M. After gassing up at the state marina in Harbor Beach, we moved our boat to our slip and were caught by a gust of wind that slammed our boat into the dock. Unfortunately, there was a piece of metal on the dock that punctured our hull about two feet above the waterline. Later that day we were able to get a diver to patch the hole in our hull with epoxy.

Harbor Beach

Harbor Beach is a small town with a state marina that is protected by a sea wall. This was the first of a number of marinas we stayed in that were run by the State of Michigan. These marinas are new and offer excellent facilities at a very reasonable price (0.75 cents per foot). The only bad news is that they do not take reservations, so it is first come, first serve. These marinas can fill up, especially on summer weekends, so I recommend you arrive before 2:00 P.M.

Harbor Beach Marina
1 Ritchie Drive
Harbor Beach, MI 48441
Phone: (517) 479-9707
www.harborbeachchamber.com/marina.html

Approach Depth	10'	Diesel Fuel	yes
Dockside Depth	10'	Mechanical Repairs	no
Accepts Transients	yes	Ships Store	yes
Dockside Power	30,50	Showers	yes
Dockside Water	yes	Laundromat	yes
Gasoline	yes	Restaurant	.5 miles

Harbor Beach to Harrisville
Chart #74 S. Lake Huron & Saginaw Bay and Chart #75 N. Lake Huron & Straits of Mackinac

The storm that was predicted veered off, and we were surprised to have good weather for our trip to Harrisville. We left the Harbor Beach

Marina and went straight out into the lake for about 6 miles, after which we went on a GPS course direct to Harrisville. Harrisville's coordinates are 44°39.5'N and 83°17'W. This course takes you across the mouth of Saginaw Bay, and you are out of sight of land most of the trip. It was a beautiful day with smooth water, and we made the trip in 3.5 hours.

Harrisville

Harrisville is a neat, clean town with a population of around 700. The Harrisville City Dock is another state-run marina with excellent new facilities and a 75-cent per foot slip fee. We had dinner in a very nice German restaurant that provided a courtesy car. Harrisville is very typical of the Lake Huron Port towns.

Harrisville City Dock, a.k.a. Harrisville Harbor of Refuge
1 Harbor Drive
Harrisville, MI 48740
Phone: (989) 724-5242

Approach Depth	12'	Diesel Fuel	yes
Dockside Depth	5'	Mechanical Repairs	no
Accepts Transients	yes	Ships Store	no
Dockside Power	30,50	Showers	yes
Dockside Water	yes	Laundromat	yes
Gasoline	yes	Restaurant	.5 miles

Harrisville to Cheboygan
Chart #75 N. Lake Huron & Straits of Mackinac

The good weather continued, with lots of sun and smooth water. We made the 91-mile trip in less than 7 hours, including a gas stop at Rogers City. We left Harrisville and went about 5 miles out into the lake, where we turned north and set our GPS course to Thunder Bay Island, which has a 63-foot tower with a horn. Your next GPS waypoints are Middle Island, with a 78-foot tower, and the Presque Island Lighthouse, 123 feet high. The next waypoint was Rogers City, where we stopped for gas, and then on to Cheboygan.

Cheboygan

Instead of staying overnight in Rogers City, we continued to Cheboygan because it is closer to Mackinac Island. Cheboygan is in the south channel portion of the Straits of Mackinac. After entering the south channel, you follow the Cheboygan Channel into the Cheboygan River. All the marinas are on the Cheboygan River. Upon entering the river, you pass the 290-foot-long Coast Guard cutter *Mackinac*, docked there. This boat is used to break up ice in late fall and early spring. We stayed at Walstrom Marina and had a good dinner at the Boathouse Restaurant, on the river.

Walstrom Marina
    113 East State Street
    Cheboygan, MI 49721
    Phone: (231) 627-7105
    e-mail: Cheboygan@walstrom.com
    www.walstrom.com

Approach Depth	25'	Diesel Fuel	no
Dockside Depth	15'	Mechanical Repairs	yes
Accepts Transients	yes	Ships Store	yes
Dockside Power	30,50	Showers	no
Dockside Water	yes	Laundromat	no
Gasoline	no	Restaurant	yes

Cheboygan to Mackinac Island
Chart #75 Lake Huron and Straits of Mackinac

We left Cheboygan at 7:00 A.M. in light rain. We cruised up the center of the South Channel for about 7 miles, then followed the shoreline of Bois Blanc Island to the west end. We continued past Round Island to Mackinac Island. We arrived in the Mackinac Island Harbor at 8:00 A.M. and immediately called the marina office on our VHF radio.

The Mackinac Island Marina is run by the State of Michigan and is the only marina on the island. This marina has only 65 slips and you cannot make a reservation. Also, this is the busiest marina in Michigan. To get into the marina, you must be in the Mackinac Island Harbor in view of the people in the marina office. You talk to them on your VHF radio and they assign a wait list number.

We were given a wait-list number of 14. We got into the marina at 1:00 P.M. This occurred on July 2^{od}; however, most other summer days would not be that crowded.

Mackinac Island

After placing our name on the waiting list, we tied up at a coal dock to wait. Since it was raining, the ladies stayed on the boat to listen on the radio for us to be called. Jim and I put on our rain gear and walked into town. At 1:00 P.M. we were called to come into the marina and the sun came out. We were put into a 40-foot slip that already housed a 20-foot boat, so our 40-foot boat stuck out by 20 feet. The Fourth of July Holiday is the busiest time of the year for the busiest marina in the State of Michigan. By rafting up and doubling up, I think they got about 100 boats into their 65-slip marina.

Mackinac Island, only reachable by ferry or your own boat, is a great place to visit. There are no automobiles on the island; all transportation is by horse and carriage or bicycle. The island is approximately three miles long and two miles wide. There is an 8-mile-long road around the perimeter of the island. We rented bicycles one morning and rode around the entire island. The island has only one village, located around the harbor. The architecture is Victorian, and with no automobiles, it looks like the 1890s. The town has several hotels and many restaurants and shops. Based on the number of fudge shops, Mackinac Island must be the fudge capital of the world.

At one end of the village is the world-famous Grand Hotel. Built in 1887, the Grand is the world's largest wooden hotel. Its front porch, more than 800 feet long, is supported by many pillars that are interspersed with flower boxes sporting red geraniums. The hotel sits on a hill with a beautiful view, and there are hundreds of white rocking chairs on the front porch. Sitting on the porch, you look down on beautiful gardens and lawn that run down to the water. People not staying at the hotel can have dinner there; however, coat and tie are required. After dinner there is dancing in an elegant ballroom with a big band.

On the hill above the village is Fort Mackinac, which took part in the war of 1812. This fort, open to the public, is very worthwhile to visit. Men in period costumes reenact eighteenth-century life in the fort.

We stayed on Mackinac Island for 4 days, including the Fourth of July. It is interesting to note that the island is so far north that it didn't get dark enough for the fireworks until 10:00 P.M.

Mackinac Island Marina
  Mackinac Island State Dock
  Mackinac Island, MI 49757
  Phone: (906) 847-3561
  www.boatingontheweb.com/mi/mackinac_island.htm

Approach Depth	10'	Diesel Fuel	no
Dockside Depth	8'	Mechanical Repairs	no
Accepts Transients	yes	Ships Store	no
Dockside Power	30	Showers	yes
Dockside Water	yes	Laundromat	yes
Gasoline	yes	Restaurant	close by

No motor-driven vehicles on Mackinac Island

MACKINAC ISLAND TO CHICAGO

LAKE MICHIGAN

CHAPTER 8

MACKINAC ISLAND TO WILMINGTON
LAKE MICHIGAN

DESTINATION	MARINA	STATUTE MILES	CUMULATIVE MILES
(DEPART MACKINAC)			
Petoskey, MI	Petoskey Municipal	50	1257
Charlevoix, MI	Northwest Marina	15	1272
Frankfort, MI	Jacobson Marina	67	1339
Pentwater, MI			
Holland, MI	Eldean Shipyard	114	1453
Benton Harbor, MI	Riverview 1000	41	1494
Chicago, IL	Burnham Park	53	1547
Wilmington, IL	Harborside Marina	55	1602

Charts Required:
Maptech ChartKit—Lake Michigan

Cruising Guide:
Lakeland Boating Ports O'Call Lake Michigan

(On the preceding page, the destinations where the author stayed are shown in bold type. These destinations are described in the following chapter. The other destinations are listed as intermediate ports if a shorter cruising day is desired. Check the cruising guide for information on intermediate ports.)

Lake Michigan

Lake Michigan is 320 miles long and varies between 50 and 118 miles wide. The lake is quite deep, with depths up to 923 feet. Summer winds are from the west; afternoon thunderstorms are common. Consequently, I recommend starting your cruise early enough to be in port before 3:00 P.M. Our cruise took us along the eastern shore of the lake, with its sandy beaches and miles and miles of large sand dunes. Behind the dunes lie many small lakes that connect to Lake Michigan by way of canals; these small lakes offer many safe harbors.

Mackinac Island to Petoskey
Maptech Chart Kit—Lake Michigan

When leaving Mackinac Island you come out of the harbor and head directly for the bridge that connects upper and lower Michigan; this bridge, one of the longest suspension bridges in the world, marks the official border between Lake Huron and Lake Michigan.

We left Mackinac Island at 7:00 A.M. on a sunny day with high winds. Unfortunately, our course for the first 25 miles was due west, into the wind. For two hours we pounded into 6-foot waves. This actually turned out to be the roughest weather we encountered on the entire trip. One crew member got sick.

It is interesting to note how important wind direction is. Our first two hours into the wind were very rough; however, when we turned south, the ride improved, and when we turned east, going into Little Traverse Bay, our travel was smooth with the wind at our back.

We arrived in Petoskey at 10:30 A.M.

Petoskey

Petoskey is at the eastern end of Little Traverse Bay. We stayed at the municipal dock, about one-half mile from downtown. The Little Traverse Historical Society Museum is adjacent to the marina. This museum has a Hemingway section; Ernest Hemingway lived in Petoskey when he was young. We had dinner at Hemingway's favorite restaurant, the Park Garden Cafe. Jim and Nancy Hoffman, who had been with us since Detroit, left us in Petoskey to fly home to Colorado. Len and Kathryn Doherty, our neighbors in Yardley, Pennsylvania, arrived several hours later. The Dohertys cruised with us to Chicago.

Petoskey Municipal Marina
100 West Lake Street
Petoskey, MI 49770
Phone: (231) 347-6691
www.fishweb.com/maps/emmet/harbors/petoskey.html

Approach Depth	10'	Diesel Fuel	no
Dockside Depth	9'	Mechanical Repairs	no
Accepts Transients	yes	Ships Store	no
Dockside Power	30	Showers	yes
Dockside Water	yes	Laundromat	no
Gasoline	yes	Restaurant	.5 miles

Petoskey to Charlevoix
Maptech ChartKit—Lake Michigan

Charlevoix is only 15 miles from Petoskey, so the whole trip was only one hour. Since the two towns are so close together, you could easily skip one or the other. We thought both towns were interesting and worthy of a visit.

Charlevoix, Michigan

Charlevoix is one of the prettiest towns on the eastern shore of Lake Michigan. Entering from Lake Michigan you pass through a short canal with houses and restaurants on either side, then under a drawbridge and into a small lake, Round Lake, that has a municipal marina. Round Lake connects to Lake Charlevoix, which is much larger. Our marina, the Northwest Marina, was on Lake Charlevoix.

Charlevoix is the home of the Belvedere Club, built before prohibition. This private club includes several hundred large, wooden summer homes of 1920s vintage, plus a private golf course, tennis courts, marina, and beach area for members only.

There are a number of good restaurants in Charlevoix. Two we especially liked were the Grey Gables, next to the Belvedere Club, and the Weather Vane Restaurant, next to the drawbridge.

Northwest Marina
Northwest Marine Yacht Basin
202 Ferry Avenue
Charlevoix, MI 49720
Phone: (231) 547-5552
www.nwmyc.com

Approach Depth	8'	Diesel Fuel	no
Dockside Depth	8'	Mechanical Repairs	yes
Accepts Transients	yes	Ships Store	yes
Dockside Power	30,50	Showers	yes
Dockside Water	yes	Laundromat	yes
Gasoline	no	Restaurant	.5 miles

Charlevoix to Frankfort
Maptech ChartKit—Lake Michigan

When NOAA issues a "small craft warning," we don't go. However, when NOAA issues a "small craft advisory," we often go if the wind is at our back. On the day we planned to go to Frankfort, we had a "small craft advisory" with south winds at 15 knots; we were headed south, so we did not go. The winds were forecasted to change to northwest the next day. The next day, the wind did shift to the northwest and the "small craft advisory" still existed, so we went to Frankfort. We had 2- to 4-foot waves but not a bad ride and it got smoother as we ran.

The course from Charlevoix to Frankfort follows the Michigan Coast South Crossing over the mouth of Grand Traverse Bay past the Grand Traverse Bay Light (50 feet high). You continue to follow the coast south to the North Manitou Shoals Light, which is 79 feet high. You then take the Manitou Passage between North and South Manitou Island and the Michigan Coast. The course is 245 and the passage is 12 miles. Next, set a course of 200, which will bring you back to the Michigan shoreline in about 15 miles; follow the shoreline from there to Frankfort.

Frankfort

Large dunes on the Michigan coast start north of Frankfort. Some are as high as 480 feet. As you come into Frankfort from the water, you go into a canal cut through the dunes. This canal leads into Betsy Lake, a safe harbor. The town and marinas are located on your left as you come through the canal.

We stayed at Jacobson Marina, one of the best marinas of the entire trip. This place had very nice built-in picnic tables and benches, plus a gas grill for every two slips. The town's main street is a block away; there you will find some nice shops and restaurants. We had dinner at the Frankfort Hotel, which featured German food and an extensive wine cellar.

Jacobson Marina
 1 4th Street
 Frankfort, MI 49635
 (231) 352-9131

Approach Depth	18'	Diesel Fuel	yes
Dockside Depth	12'	Mechanical Repairs	yes
Accepts Transients	yes	Ships Store	yes
Dockside Power	30,50	Showers	yes
Dockside Water	yes	Laundromat	yes
Gasoline	yes	Restaurant	yes

Frankfort to Holland
 Maptech ChartKit—Lake Michigan

We had originally planned to go from Frankfort to Pentwater to stay the night and then onto Holland. However, since we spent an extra day in Charlevoix, we decided to make it up by going from Frankfort to Holland in one day. The four of us had airplane tickets home from Chicago and we didn't want to cut our time in Chicago short. The other reason for our decision was that the weather was beautiful and the lake was flat.

We simply followed the coastline 2 to 3 miles off the whole way. However, I always program our waypoints into the GPS, which gives you "miles to go" and "time to go" as well as course corrections at the end. In this case, I programmed both Pentwater and Holland, since we planned to stop in Pentwater for gas.

We left Frankfort at 8:00 A.M. and were in Pentwater by noon. We arrived in Holland by 4:00 P.M., having traveled 114 miles that day.

Holland

Holland is another town on a lake behind the sand dunes. After coming through the short canal into the lake, you turn right into the Eldean Shipyard, a very nice marina with a gourmet restaurant overlooking all the boats. The town of Holland is located at the other end of Lake Macatawa, which is 5 miles long.

Holland, originally settled by the Dutch, is famous for their annual Tulip Festival in May. On the outskirts of town are two wooden-shoe factories and a tulip farm you can visit.

Eldean Shipyard Marina
2223 S. Shore Drive
Macatawa, MI 49434
Phone: (616) 335-5843
www.eldean.com/Marina_Services/Contact_Us/contact_us.html

Approach Depth	20'	Diesel Fuel	yes
Dockside Depth	17'	Mechanical Repairs	yes
Accepts Transients	yes	Ships Store	yes
Dockside Power	30,50	Showers	yes
Dockside Water	yes	Laundromat	yes
Gasoline	yes	Restaurant	yes

Holland to Benton Harbor
Maptech ChartKit—Lake Michigan

The trip from Holland to Benton Harbor is only 41 miles down the Michigan coastline. We arrived in time for lunch. The weather continued good.

Benton Harbor

Benton Harbor and its neighboring town of St. Joseph are industrial towns, and the only reason for going there is that the trip across the lake to Chicago is only 53 miles. You can skip this port and go directly to Chicago from Holland, but that trip is 90 miles. Since we didn't know what the weather would be, we opted for the shorter trip.

  I'm sure that one of these towns has a nice restaurant, but the one we went to was mediocre. In retrospect, this would have been a good place to have dinner on board.

Riverview 1000 Marina
  1000 Riverview Drive
  Benton Harbor, MI 49022
  Phone: (269) 927-4471
  www.pier1000.com

Approach Depth	6'	Diesel Fuel	yes
Dockside Depth	6'	Mechanical Repairs	yes
Accepts Transients	yes	Ships Store	yes
Dockside Power	30,50	Showers	yes
Dockside Water	yes	Laundromat	yes
Gasoline	yes	Restaurant	taxi ride

Benton Harbor to Chicago
Maptech ChartKit—Lake Michigan

We made the 53-mile crossing from Benton Harbor to Chicago in 3 hours. The weather continued good, and we had a smooth ride. We could see the tops of the Chicago skyscrapers from 20 miles out—in particular, the Sears Tower. The Chicago skyline from the lake is a spectacular sight.

Chicago

> **Chicago lakefront is unique because the city of Chicago owns and operates marine facilities on the lakefront. Now Westrec Marine manages these harbors and private yacht clubs operate on the property.**

We stayed at the Burnham Park Municipal Marina, which I strongly recommend because of its location. This marina is run by the City of Chicago and is quite large. They do not have transient slips as such; however, if you call them several days in advance, they will assign you a slip that will be empty during your stay. The marina is located in a protected body of water with a small-plane airport (due to become a park) on the lakeside, and the McCormick Place and Soldier Field on the city side. Adjacent to the north end of the marina is the Adler Planetarium, the Shedd Aquarium, and the Field Museum of Natural History. Also in front of the aquarium is a very busy taxi stand and a place to get tour buses of the city.

Chicago has much to do, but we were there for only three days. We visited all the museums within walking distance, and we took the open trolley tour of the city.

Burnham Park Municipal Harbor
    1559 S. Lake Shore Drive
    Chicago, IL 60605
    Phone: (312) 747-7009 (regular season) or (312) 742-8520 (off
    season)
    www.chicagoharbors.info

Approach Depth	20'	Diesel Fuel	yes
Dockside Depth	15'	Mechanical Repairs	no
Accepts Transients	yes	Ships Store	no
Dockside Power	30,50	Showers	yes
Dockside Water	yes	Laundromat	yes
Gasoline	yes	Restaurant	no

The Illinois Waterway

Starting at Lake Michigan with the Chicago River, the next stretch of waterway is the Chicago Sanitary and Ship Canal that joins the Des Plaines River to form the Illinois Waterway. From Calumet Harbor, south of Chicago, the Calumet River joins the Chicago Sanitary and Ship Canal. The waterway flows southwest to the Mississippi River (Mile 217.0) at Grafton, IL about 20 miles north of St. Louis. Once inside the Chicago Lock or the O'Brien Lock (on the Calumet River), seven more locks on the Illinois Waterway will lower your boat from 580-foot elevation at Lake Michigan to 433-foot elevation at Grafton. Red nun buoys are located on the left descending bank and black can buoys are on the right. Many lights and daymarks, established along riverbanks, give the mile at that location.

Chicago to Wilmington, Illinois

There are a number of fixed bridges on the Illinois Waterway; however, the two lowest are a 17-foot clearance on the Chicago River (MM320.4) and a 19-foot clearance at mile 300.2 after the Calumet and Chicago Sanitary and Ship Canal come together. If you can clear the 17-foot bridge, you can take the Chicago River through downtown Chicago from Lake Michigan; otherwise, you must take the Calumet River at Calumet Harbor from Lake Michigan. In both cases you still have to clear the 19-foot bridge.

I recommend you start this trip early, since the speed limit is 6 mph all through Chicago and there are a number of lift bridges that you have to wait for. After coming through the city of Chicago, about 36 miles from the lake is the Lockport Lock at Mile 291. The next lock, only 5 miles away, is the Brandon Road Lock at Mile 286 Wilmington, Illinois. The Harborside Marina is at Mile 273.7. You are now traveling through rural farm areas. This 55-mile trip took us 8 hours.

The Illinois Waterway consists of several channels that connect Lake Michigan to the Mississippi River at Grafton, Illinois. The sequence is either the Chicago River near Navy Pier in Chicago to the South Branch to the Sanitary Ship Canal
or the Calumet River to the Little Calumet River, the Calumet Sag Channel and join the Chicago Sanitary Ship Canal to the Des Plaines River to the Illinois River. Enter the system either in Chicago at the Chicago Lock (MM327) or at Calumet River (MM333) through the Thomas O'Brien Lock. There are seven more locks: Lockport (290.0), Brandon (286.0), Dresden (271.5), Marseilles (244.6), Starved Rock (234.1), Peoria (157.7) and La Grange (80.2) before entering the Mississippi River. Peoria and La Grange

locks are wicket dams; during high water, the wickets are lowered and traffic passes over the dam without passing through the lock. Entering the waterway at the Chicago, boats must clear 17-feet overhead clearance. Using the alternative, Calumet River, the allowable overhead clearance increases to 24 feet; however, the 19-foot fixed bridge is at Mile 300.6.

Bick's text as rewritten by Laura:

There are two routes from Lake Michigan to the Illinois Waterway, the Calumet River or Chicago River. We took the Chicago River that has spectacular views since it goes through downtown Chicago past numerous skyscrapers and under numerous bridges. The lowest fixed bridge is 17 feet at normal pool stage. (The lowest fixed bridge on the waterway is listed as 19.1 feet at Mile 300.6. I recommend you start this trip early since the speed limit is 6 mph all through Chicago and you might have to wait for several bridges to open. About 36 miles from the lake is Lockport Lock, Mile 291. The next lock, Brandon Road, is 5 miles downstream at Mile 286. Our destination, Harborside Marina at Wilmington, IL in a rural setting, is at Mile 273.7. Running time for this 55-mile trip was 8 hours. My wife and I left our boat at Harborside Marina and flew home.

Harborside Marina [MM 273.7]
   Phone: (815) 476-2254

Accepts Transients	yes	Mechanical Repairs	yes
Dockside Power	30,50	Ships Store	yes
Dockside Water	yes	Showers	yes
Gasoline	yes	Laundromat	no
Diesel Fuel	yes	Restaurant	yes

Caution: The navigable channel on the Illinois Waterway is 9 feet deep. Wing dams are submerged piles of material that prevent erosion and are usually beneath the water surface; however, there are times during low water when they are visible. Occasionally buoys are moved off station when struck by a barge.

Marina at Frankfort, Michigan

Marina in downtown Chicago next to Soldier Field

Entering the Chicago River from Lake Michigan

WILMINGTON TO THE TENN-TOM CANAL

ILLINOIS, MISSISSIPPI, OHIO, AND TENNESSEE RIVERS

CHAPTER 9

WILMINGTON TO THE TENN-TOM CANAL
ILLINOIS, MISSISSIPPI, OHIO, AND TENNESSEE RIVERS

DESTINATION	MARINA	STATUTE MILES	CUMULATIVE MILES
(Depart Wilmington)			
Henry, IL	Henry Harbor Marina	78	1680
Pekin, IL			
Browning, IL	Rivers Edge Boat Club	99	1779
Naples, IL			
Portage des Sioux, MO	My River Home	104	1883
Ste. Genevieve, MO	Marina de Gabouri	90	1973
Cairo, IL (anchorage)		121	2094
Grand Rivers, KY	Green Turtle Bay	83	2177
Buchanan, TN			
Waverly, KY	Cuba Landing	92	2269
Saltillo, TN			
Iuka, MS	Aqua Yacht Harbor	104	2373

Charts Required:
U. S. Army Corps of Engineers Charts
Charts of the Illinois Waterway
Upper Mississippi River Navigation Charts
Ohio River Navigation Charts—Cairo, IL to Foster, KY
Tennessee River Navigation Charts

Cruising Guide:
Quimby's Cruising Guide

(On the preceding page, the destinations where the author stayed are shown in bold type. These destinations are described in the following chapter. The other destinations are listed as intermediate ports if a shorter cruising day is desired. Check the cruising guide for information on intermediate ports.)

Wilmington, Illinois to Henry, Illinois

This section of the trip (Chicago to the Tenn-Tom Canal) had some special problems that I will discuss later. For this reason my crew for this section of the trip was Charlie Frame, a captain with extensive experience. Charlie and I returned to Harborside Marina on September 9, 1996 to resume the trip.

The trip from Wilmington to Henry, Illinois is 78 miles long and includes three locks where there can be considerable delays. I recommend that you get an early start on this day, even though you will be able to go at cruising speeds most of the time. On the Erie Canal the boat traffic is recreational, so there are very seldom long delays at locks. However, the major traffic on the Illinois Waterway is barge traffic, and they have the preference at locks.

The Illinois River and the Mississippi River have very heavy barge traffic; you will see a tow going either upbound or downbound every 10 to 15 minutes. When you see a tow, you contact them on your VHF radio to ask on which side they want you to pass them.

The western rivers' whistle signals when boats are passing are: one blast means "I intend to leave you on my port side," and two blasts means "I intend to leave you on my starboard side." It is common practice not to blow the whistle but rather to ask the tug captain on the radio which he prefers, "one or two whistles?" All tows move at 6 mph, so slow down to 8 mph when passing them.

First is Dresdon Lock and Dam. Second is the Marseilles Lock at Mile 244.6. The third is the Starved Rock Lock at Mile 231. We did not have any delays at these two locks, but averaged about 30 minutes per lock.

Henry, Illinois is at Mile 196. The trip is quite scenic, passing through farmland and small towns. We stayed at the Henry Harbor Marina, which has a motel and restaurant.

Henry Harbor Marina (MM 196.1)
210 Cromwell Drive
Henry, IL 61537
Phone: (309) 364-2181
www.peoriaboats.com/MarinasHTML/henry.html

Accepts Transients	yes	Mechanical Repairs	no
Dockside Power	30	Ships Store	no
Dockside Water	yes	Showers	yes
Gasoline	yes	Laundromat	no
Diesel Fuel	yes	Restaurant	yes

Henry, Illinois to Browning, Illinois

The trip from Henry to Browning is 99 miles and includes 1 lock at Peoria (Mile 157.7). Peoria is known for the Par-A-Dice, a 228-foot-long stern-wheeler riverboat casino. We passed the Par-A-Dice, which was under way as we went through Peoria.

We had another interesting experience in the Peoria Lock. When we got to the lock, a tow was waiting to go in. Since this tow was only going to use half of the lock, we called the lockmaster on the radio and asked if we could lock through with the tow. The lockmaster, in this case, must ask the tow captain for his permission, and he said yes, so we moved into the lock after the tow boat.

Our normal practice when in a lock is to hold our boat to the side of the lock by looping the lock lines under a cleat and then playing out the line as our boat descends. We learned that when you are in a lock with a *tow*, you must tie the lock line tight to the cleat as soon as the boat reaches the lower water level, for when the tow starts its powerful engines, the backwash against the rear gate causes severe turbulence. We were not tied tight to our cleats, so the turbulence blew our boat away from the wall.

Browning, Illinois is a small town of approximately 200, including cats and dogs. The main industry, believe it or not, is fishing. These people fish the Illinois River for buffalo, carp, and catfish with nets, using open boats 24 feet long by 8 feet wide. We talked to one fisherman we met at the restaurant at the River's Edge Boat Club. He told us that he and his partner catch 10 tons of fish per week. They go out each morning until their open boat is filled with fish. They then pull their boat filled with fish onto a trailer and haul it to a wholesale fish dealer. Most of this type of fish is used for cat food.

The River's Edge Boat Club is a restaurant on pilings at the river's edge; it has a barge containing gas and diesel pumps. We tied up to the gas barge for the night. The restaurant had a $5.00, all-you-can-eat, fish dinner featuring the local fish. The catfish was ok, but we didn't like the buffalo or the carp.

River's Edge Boat Club (MM 97.5 RDB)
Route 100 and Walnut Street
Browning, IL 62624
Phone: (217) 323-4780

Accepts Transients	yes	Mechanical Repairs	no
Dockside Power	no	Ships Store	no
Dockside Water	no	Showers	no
Gasoline	yes	Laundromat	no
Diesel Fuel	yes	Restaurant	yes

Browning, Illinois to Portage des Sioux, Missouri

The trip from Browning, Illinois to the Mississippi is 97.5 miles with one lock, the La Grange Lock, at Mile Marker 80.2. The scenery is farmland and beautiful countryside. The last 6 miles of today's trip was on the Mississippi. We stayed at My River Home Harbor Marina at the town of Portage des Sioux on the Missouri side of the river.

Portage des Sioux is at Mississippi River Mile Marker 212.4 and is 32 miles north of downtown St. Louis. There are several marinas in this area, but there are no marinas and no docks in St. Louis. You either stay 32 miles north or 22 miles south of St. Louis at Hoppies Marina in Kimmswick, Missouri.

My River Home Harbor (MM212.4 RDB)
1545 Riverview Drive
Portage des Sioux, MO 63373
Phone: (314) 899-0903
www.myriverhome.com

Accepts Transients	yes	Mechanical Repairs	yes
Dockside Power	30	Ships Store	yes
Dockside Water	yes	Showers	yes
Gasoline	yes	Laundromat	yes
Diesel Fuel	yes	Restaurant	yes

The Alton Marina is now located at mile 202.9 on the Upper Mississippi River, LDB, making the trip to Portage des Sioux unnecessary.

The Alton Marina
Phone: (618) 462-9860
Transients, Gas/Diesel, Pool, Restrooms/Shower, Laundry, Ships Store/Groceries, Pump Out, Repairs, walk to Restaurant/Shopping, Courtesy Shuttle, 18 ton Haul-out. Open year round.

St. Louis, Missouri

If you wish to go sightseeing in St. Louis, you will need to rent a car to get from the marina to downtown St. Louis. The Gateway Arch is the most famous monument on the Mississippi and at 630 feet tall is the tallest in the U.S. A tram system carries visitors to the observation room at the top. A museum and a theater are at the bottom. St. Louis has some excellent museums and a famous botanical garden and zoo. St. Louis also has many good restaurants and riverboat gambling.

The Mississippi River

The Mississippi River is divided into two parts, namely the Upper Mississippi and the Lower Mississippi. The Upper Mississippi starts in Minneapolis and runs 858 miles to Cairo, Illinois, where the Ohio River joins the Mississippi. The Upper Mississippi is more scenic than the Lower and has marinas to service recreational boating.

The Lower Mississippi goes from Cairo, Illinois to New Orleans, Louisiana, a total of 856 miles. The Lower Mississippi has few harbors and long distances between gas stops. Barge traffic is very heavy and there is very little recreational boating. The current in the Mississippi can be 6 mph in the spring and average 2 to 4 mph normally. The Mississippi is also known for floating debris that can be as large as a telephone pole. For all of these reasons, I recommend that you leave the Mississippi at Cairo, Illinois and take the alternative Tenn-Tom route to the Gulf. If you take the Tenn-Tom route, you will be on the Mississippi for 218 miles from where the Illinois River joins the Mississippi to Cairo, Illinois, Upper Mississippi Mile 0.

> Since there are few marinas on the Lower Mississippi, most pleasure boats travel the Ohio River (past the Tennessee River junction, avoiding the Kentucky Lock on the Tennessee River), to the Cumberland River, through the Barkley Lock to Green Turtle Bay Marina. There is a cut to the Tennessee River to continue downbound.

Portage des Sioux to Ste. Genevieve, Missouri

The trip from Portage des Sioux (Upper Mississippi Mile 212) to Ste. Genevieve, Missouri is 90 miles. (As a point of reference, the famous St. Louis Gateway Arch, especially impressive from the water, is at Mile 180.) We had a 3-mph current in our favor, so we made good time.

Between Portage des Sioux and Ste. Genevieve there are two locks: MelPrice Lock and Dam, Mile 200.8, and Chain of Rocks Lock and Dam, Mile 185.0.

Tows on the Illinois River are large; however, tows on the Mississippi are even larger. We saw many tows that were three barges wide and several that were four barges wide. All barges seem to be a standard size of 25 feet wide by 50 feet long. I am told that each barge holds the equivalent of 50 eighteen-wheeler trucks. Therefore, a tow 3 barges wide by 5 long would carry as much material as 750 trucks.

Marina de Gabouri in Ste. Genevieve, Missouri is in a little cove out of the Mississippi current. The marina is basically a gas dock; on the day we were there, four boats, all in the 30- to 40-foot size, used up all the dock space.

On the entire trip we never met another boat that was on the Great Circle Cruise, except on this day. All three of the other boats at this marina were on the Great Circle Cruise and were traveling together. These boats had started in Florida in April 1996 and would finish in November seven months later. We would see these boats again at our anchorage at Cairo, Illinois and at our next marina, on the Cumberland River.

Staying at this particular marina is strategically important, since it offers the last gas for 175 miles and the last marina for 204 miles. This created a special problem for us, because we only have a range of 120 miles when cruising at 18 mph. (Boats with diesel engines have much longer ranges; for them, this would not be a problem.) Our plan was to run at 10 mph for the 121 miles to Cairo, Illinois to conserve fuel. Since we had a 3-mph current in our favor, we would actually make 13-mph speed over ground. At Cairo, Illinois, we would anchor out for the night and add 50 gallons of gas from 10 five-gallon gas cans that we carried on our aft deck. The next day we would cruise up the Ohio River 53 miles to the gas dock. Even though we would be bucking the current on the Ohio River, we calculated that 50 gallons extra should be enough.

Marina de Gabouri
 1 Marina Drive
 Ste. Genevieve, MO 63670
 Phone: (573) 883-5599

Accepts Transients	yes	Mechanical Repairs	no
Dockside Power	30,50	Ships Store	yes
Dockside Water	yes	Showers	yes
Gasoline	yes	Laundromat	no
Diesel Fuel	yes	Restaurant	yes

Ste. Genevieve, Missouri to Cairo, Illinois

About a month before flying back to Chicago to resume the trip, I ordered 10 five-gallon gas cans from Boat/US and had them shipped to Marina de Gabouri. The marina held them for me until our arrival, so we didn't have to store them on the boat.

When we arrived at the marina, the gas pump was broken and they were working to fix it. Unfortunately, they didn't get the gas pump fixed until 10 A.M. the next morning. By the time we filled our gas tanks with 240 gallons and filled the 10 gas cans with another 50 gallons, it was 11:00 A.M. In retrospect, we should have waited until the next morning to leave, but we didn't.

Since we were traveling at the slow speed of 10 mph through the water, it got dark before we arrived at our anchorage at Cairo, Illinois. We had a built-in searchlight on the boat that could be moved with four buttons. This turned out to be almost worthless in trying to spot markers on the very dark Mississippi River. We should have had a handheld halogen light that operates from the cigarette lighter at the helm with a 12-foot flexible cord. The next time we were caught running in the dark, we had the halogen light; this worked great to find the channel. We arrived at our anchorage after an hour of running in the dark and guessing where the channel was.

The anchorage was in a cove, out of the Mississippi current on the Illinois side and on the north side of the bridge that crosses the Mississippi at Cairo, Illinois. The three boats that were also on the Great Circle Cruise were diesel and, therefore, had been unaffected by the gas pump problem. When we arrived at the anchorage, the three boats were already anchored there. We anchored out for the night, and the next morning we put 25 gallons into each of our two tanks.

> Since no fuel or dockage is available on the Ohio River between mile 981 and 922.8 (Cumberland River junction), it is important to plan this part of the trip with extreme care. Passing the Tennessee River junction in favor of the Cumberland River is highly recommended. Heavy traffic at the Kentucky Lock can cause long delays.

Cairo, Illinois to Grand Rivers, Kentucky

We had 53 miles to go on the Ohio River to get gas. The gas dock [no longer available] was at Ohio Mile 928.4, and the Tennessee River is at Ohio Mile 934.2. The Ohio River starts with Mile 0.0 in Pittsburgh, Pennsylvania and ends at Cairo, Illinois, Ohio Mile 981. What this means is that we had to go 6 miles past the Tennessee River to get gas and then come back those 6 miles to the Tennessee River. Since we were bucking the current on the Ohio, we covered only about 15 miles when cruising at 18 mph through the water.

We recommend bypassing Tennessee River to junction of Cumberland River through Barkley Lock to Green Turtle Bay Marina (MM32) on Cumberland River.

There were two locks on the Ohio River; one at Ohio Mile 962.6, and the second at Mile 938.9. When we got to the gas dock, we filled both tanks, and I calculated that if we had not carried the extra 50 gallons, we would have been 16 gallons short of making the gas dock. I gave the empty gas cans to the lady at the gas dock and she was very appreciative. I did not want to carry 10 used empty gas cans on the boat.

We left the gas dock and went 6 miles to the Tennessee River and then 21 miles up the Tennessee River to the Kentucky Lock. The Kentucky Lock has a lift of 57 feet; it uses floating bollards to tie your boat to in the lock. The floating bollard makes it much easier to hold your boat to the side of the lock using only one line between a mid-cleat on your boat and the bollard.

We were very lucky: just as we got to the Kentucky Lock they were taking pleasure boats into the lock. We found out that some of those boats had been waiting for four hours. Commercial traffic has the right-of-way at these locks, so if there is commercial traffic, the pleasure boats have to wait. When you come through the lock there is a large marina on the Tennessee River; however, the Green Turtle Bay Marina, two miles away on the Cumberland River, had been recommended to us, so we went there. It turned out to be a good choice. They had a yacht club that accepted transients for dinner. We stayed there several days to relax.

Green Turtle Bay Marina (MM32 Cumberland River)
263 Green Turtle Bay Drive
Grand Rivers, KY 42055
Phone: (270) 362-8364
www.greenturtlebay.com

Accepts Transients	yes	Mechanical Repairs	yes
Dockside Power	30,50	Ships Store	yes
Dockside Water	yes	Showers	yes
Gasoline	yes	Laundromat	yes
Diesel Fuel	yes	Restaurant	yes

Grand Rivers, Kentucky to Waverly, Tennessee

The Tennessee is a beautiful river, especially the part that we traveled on this trip, known as the Kentucky Lake. Kentucky Lake is a 180-mile-long part of the Tennessee River between the Kentucky Dam and the Pickwick Dam. This long lake has five state parks and 80 resorts on its shores. At its northern end is The Land Between The Lakes, a very large resort area run by the Tennessee Valley Authority.

Our trip to Waverly, Tennessee and Cuba Landing Marina was 92 miles and was all beautiful lake. We only saw about one tow per hour, as compared to the Mississippi's one tow every 10 minutes.

Cuba Landing Marina had just been rebuilt, with new docks, ships store, etc., in 1996. They lent us a courtesy van and Charlie and I went to a restaurant and had chicken-fried steak.

Cuba Landing Marina (MM 115.5 RDB Tennessee River)
302 Cuba Marina Lane
Waverly, TN 37185
Phone: (931) 296-2822

Accepts Transients	yes	Mechanical Repairs	yes
Dockside Power	30,50	Ships Store	yes
Dockside Water	yes	Showers	yes
Gasoline	yes	Laundromat	yes
Diesel Fuel	yes	Restaurant	no

Waverly, Tennessee to Iuka, Mississippi

The trip to Iuka, Mississippi is 104 miles; the first 91 miles is on Kentucky Lake to the Pickwick Lock and Dam. Pickwick Lock has a lift of 55 feet and is at Tennessee Mile 206.7.

After going through the lock, you continue on the Tennessee River for about 8 miles to the junction with the Tenn-Tom Waterway (Tennessee Mile 215 and Tenn-Tom Mile 452). Following the Tenn-Tom, the Aqua Yacht Harbor is only 4 miles away. Aqua Yacht Harbor is quite large, including swimming pool, tennis court, restaurant, and courtesy vans.

Charlie Frame got a ride to Memphis and flew home to Philadelphia on Thursday. My wife, Jeri, and our friends, George and Anaruth Hynson, were not scheduled to arrive from Memphis until Sunday so I had three days alone where I didn't have to move the boat, which was relaxing. I borrowed the courtesy car and visited the Shiloh Battlefield Park on one day, an excursion I would recommend.

Aqua Yacht Harbor (MM 448.7 RDB Tombigbee)
 3832 Hwy. 25N
 Iuka, MS 38852
 Phone: (601) 423-2222
 www.aquayachtharbor.com

Accepts Transients	yes	Mechanical Repairs	yes
Dockside Power	30,50	Ships Store	yes
Dockside Water	yes	Showers	yes
Gasoline	yes	Laundromat	yes
Diesel Fuel	yes	Restaurant	yes

A tow pushing into a lock on the Illinois River

Nittany Navy docked on the Illinois River

Approaching St. Louis in the Mississippi

The Mississippi Queen

Tenn-Tom Canal to Mobile, Alabama

Tenn-Tom Waterway System

← *Tennessee River*

TENNESSEE

• Pickwick, TN

☆ Smithville Marina

← *Tombigbee Waterway*

☆ Marina Cove

ALABAMA
← *Black Warrior River*

☆ Demopolis Yacht Basin

☆ Lady's Landing

← *Alabama River*

MISSISSIPPI

New Orleans, LA

☆ Grand Mariner Marina
• Mobile, AL
• Pensacola, FL

LOUISIANA

Gulf of Mexico

CHAPTER 10

TENN-TOM CANAL TO MOBILE, ALABAMA
TENN-TOM WATERWAY SYSTEM

DESTINATION	MARINA	STATUTE MILES	CUMULATIVE MILES
(Depart Iuka, MS)			
Bay Springs, AL	Smithville Marina	72	2445
Carrolton, AL	Marina Cove	69	2514
Demopolis, AL	Demopolis Yacht Basin	91	2605
Bashi Creek, AL	(Anchorage)		
Jackson, AL	Lady's Landing	137	2742
Mobile, AL	Grand Mariner Marina	87	2829

Charts Required:
  U. S. Army Corps of Engineers Charts
    Tennessee-Tombigbee Waterway Charts
    Lower Black Warrior-Tombigbee Waterway Charts
Cruising Guide:
    Quimby's Cruising Guide

Destinations where the author stayed, shown here in bold type, are described in the following chapter. The other destinations are listed as intermediate ports if a shorter cruising day is desired. Check the cruising guide for information on intermediate ports.

The Tenn-Tom Waterway

The Tenn-Tom Waterway connects the Tennessee River in Mississippi to the Lower Black Warrior River in Alabama. This waterway system provides a parallel route to the lower Mississippi when traveling from the upper Mississippi to the Gulf. The Waterway system is 450 miles long and has 12 locks. The system lowers your boat from an elevation of 341 feet at the Tennessee River to sea level at Mobile, Alabama. As previously stated, this is a much more pristine and relaxing way to cruise to the Gulf than taking the lower Mississippi.

The canal project was started in 1972 and completed in 1985. It was the largest project ever undertaken by the Army Corps of Engineers, costing 2 billion dollars. The amount of dirt moved exceeded that moved to create the Panama Canal.

The 12 locks are all 600 feet long by 110 feet wide and are of the latest design, using floating bollards to tie up to when in the lock. The floating bollards are built into the sides of the lock and float up and down with the water level. You only need to tie one line from a center cleat on your boat to the floating bollard to hold your boat to the side of the lock.

The Tenn-Tom Waterway has more recreational boats than commercial boats and is the main route in spring and fall for recreational boats traveling between the Mid-West and Florida.

The Waterway system travels through extremely rural sections of Mississippi and Alabama. During our trip down the Tenn-Tom, we passed hundreds of bass boats and quite a few duck hunters in their camouflaged boats.

> **Boaters should be alert. Watch for camouflaged locals who are fishing and hunting. Create no wakes that might disturb them.**

Iuka, Mississippi to Smithville, Mississippi

Our first day on the Tenn-Tom we went 72 miles and passed through 4 locks. The Tenn-Tom was prettier than we expected, with very little barge or boat traffic at all. Since it was late September, many of the boats we saw were going in our direction and were headed for Florida.

At the third lock, Lock D, a 55-foot Viking pulled out of the lock in front of us out of turn. We followed in their wake at 18 knots until we came to the Midway Marina and slowed down; however, the Viking did not slow down.

When we got to the fourth lock, Lock C, the police were waiting for the Viking. When the lock opened, we followed the Viking into the lock and tied up to a floating bollard. The police came over to the Viking and asked the captain to get off the boat. They arrested the captain and took him away in a police car.

We talked to the police before we left the lock and they said that the Viking had caused possibly $2,000 worth of damage at the Midway Marina. We followed the Viking, with someone else piloting, to the Smithville Marina. Several hours later, the captain of the Viking arrived at the marina. He had had a hearing before a Justice Of The Peace and posted an $800 bond to assure his appearance in their court at a later date. The people at the Smithville Marina told us that the Midway Marina was famous for having people arrested who didn't slow down when going past their marina.

We borrowed Smithville Marina's courtesy car and went into Smithville to buy food to eat on our boat. The only food available was catfish, barbecue, ribs, and chicken. The food was good; however, we found out that for the next four nights the only food available from local restaurants were the same four things. After several nights we had had enough of the local cuisine, so we switched to food we carried on board.

Smithville Marina, MM 377.0 LDB Tombigbee
60036 Marina Trl
Smithville, MS 38870
Phone: (662) 651-4334

Approach Depth	10'	Diesel Fuel	yes
Dockside Depth	7'	Mechanical Repairs	no
Accepts Transients	yes	Ships Store	no
Dockside Power	30,50	Showers	yes
Dockside Water	yes	Laundromat	yes
Gasoline	yes	Restaurant	no

Smithville, Mississippi to Carrolton, Alabama

The second day on the Tenn-Tom we went 69 miles and did 4 locks. The scenery continued to be beautiful, and because of the dams, the water is very tranquil. We stayed at the Marina Cove Marina in Carrolton, Alabama. This marina is located only one mile from the Tom Bevell lock and museum. The museum is a beautiful reproduction of a southern mansion and is a shrine to Tom Bevell, who as an Alabama Congressman and chairman of the Waterways Subcommittee, got the money to build the Tenn-Tom Waterway. The museum is quite interesting and documents building the waterway.

The restaurants in Carrolton are only open on Thursday, Friday, and Saturday. We were there on a Tuesday, so we bought barbecue and took it to the boat. The entire region through which the waterway runs seems to be "dry" counties in Mississippi and Alabama. If you like to have beer or wine with dinner, be sure to bring it with you before you start the Tenn-Tom.

Marina Cove Marina
595 Marina Parkway
Carrollton, AL 35447
Phone: (205) 373-6701

Approach Depth	9'	Diesel Fuel	yes
Dockside Depth	7'	Mechanical Repairs	no
Accepts Transients	yes	Ships Store	no
Dockside Power	30,50	Showers	yes
Dockside Water	yes	Laundromat	yes
Gasoline	yes	Restaurant	no

Carrolton, Alabama to Demopolis, Alabama

The third day on the Tenn-Tom we went 91 miles and passed through 2 locks. We continued to be amazed by the small amount of boat traffic, both pleasure and commercial. The tows are small compared to the Mississippi River. The typical tows on the Tenn-Tom were only 2 to 6 barges per tow. Demopolis is at the junction with the Black Warrior River; this is approximately the halfway point on the waterway and where you change chart books. The Demopolis Yacht Basin was the marina where we stayed. The marina was large for the Tenn-Tom and had a restaurant and bar. The tows stop at the Demopolis Yacht Basin to refuel, which takes some hours since the tows can carry several thousand gallons of diesel fuel.

Demopolis Yacht Basin (Lower Black Warrior 217.7 LDB)
Highway 43 North
Demopolis, AL 36732
Phone: (334) 289-4647
www.demyb.com

Approach Depth	18'		Diesel Fuel	yes
Dockside Depth	18'		Mechanical Repairs	yes
Accepts Transients	yes		Ships Store	yes
Dockside Power	30,50		Showers	yes
Dockside Water	yes		Laundromat	yes
Gasoline	yes		Restaurant	yes

Demopolis, Alabama to Lady's Landing, Alabama

The trip from Demopolis to Lady's Landing is 137 miles with 2 locks. This can be done in one or two days with an anchorage, since there are no marinas between these two points. If you wish to make the trip in two days, you can anchor out at Bashi Creek, 72 miles from Demopolis. Alternately, if you choose to do the 137 miles in one day as we did, you can get gas at Bobby's Fish Camp, 98 miles from Demopolis. Bobby's Fish Camp does not have any overnight docking.

> Bobby's Fish Camp [Mile 118.9 RDB] does have dockage, a restaurant, limited groceries, and other amenities.

Lady's Landing, Alabama to Mobile, Alabama

It is 80 miles from Lady's Landing to downtown Mobile, plus another 7 miles to Dog River where all the marinas are. The last 20 miles before Mobile, the river gradually widens into Mobile Bay. Downtown Mobile is quite impressive, with new, modern buildings and a busy port.

Mobile, Alabama

We stayed at the Grand Mariner Marina [Mobile Bay at Dog River], which had a good seafood restaurant on the premises. One of their specialties was big red shrimp steamed in Old Bay Seasoning. You peel the shrimp and dip them in butter. They were so good, I had them twice as a dinner.

We rented a car from Enterprise, since we were about 8 miles from downtown Mobile. The second day in Mobile it rained all day, so we stayed on the boat and watched Penn State beat Wisconsin in a "squeaker." The next morning we took George and Anaruth Hynson to the airport. That night, Jeri and I had dinner at NanSeas, a very nice waterfront restaurant close to the marina.

The next day we picked up our next crew at the Mobile Airport: our son, Scott, and his wife, Bonnie. They would go with us to New Orleans.

Grand Mariner Marina
    6036 Rock Point Road
    Mobile, AL 36605-9777
    Phone: (251) 443-6300
    www.grand-marinermarina.com

Approach Depth	15'	Diesel Fuel	yes
Dockside Depth	15'	Mechanical Repairs	yes
Accepts Transients	yes	Ships Store	yes
Dockside Power	30,50	Showers	yes
Dockside Water	yes	Laundromat	yes
Gasoline	yes	Restaurant	yes

The proper way to tie from a mid-cleat to a floating bollard
in a Tenn-Tom lock

Fishermen in the Tenn-Tom

White Cliffs on the Tenn-Tom

Mobile, Alabama waterfront

Mobile to New Orleans
to Cedar Key, Florida

Gulf Intracoastal Waterway

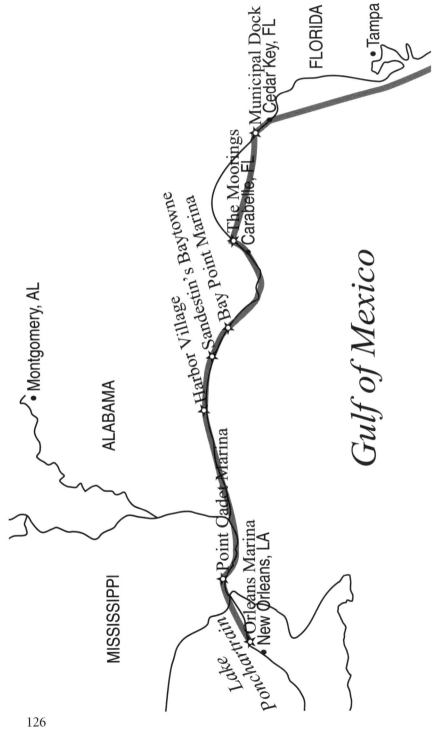

CHAPTER 11

MOBILE TO NEW ORLEANS TO CEDAR KEY
GULF INTRACOASTAL WATERWAY

DESTINATION	MARINA	STATUTE MILES	CUMULATIVE MILES
(Depart Mobile)			
Biloxi, MS	Point Cadet Marina	85	2914
Bay St. Louis, MO			
New Orleans, LA	Orleans Marina	106	3020
Biloxi, MS	Point Cadet Marina	106	3126
Pensacola, FL	Harbor Village	97	3223
Destin, FL	Sandestin's Baytowne	30	3253
Panama City, FL	Bay Point Marina	45	3298
Carrabelle, FL	The Moorings	80	3378
Cedar Key, FL	Municipal Dock	120	3498

Charts Required:
    NOAA Charts: 11376, 11378, 11385
    Maptech ChartKits
        Florida's West Coast and the Keys

Cruising Guide:
    Waterway Guide—Southern

The destinations where the author stayed, shown in bold type, are described in the following chapter. The other destinations are listed as intermediate ports if a shorter cruising day is desired. Check the cruising guide for information on intermediate ports.

The Gulf Intracoastal Waterway (GIWW)

The Gulf Intracoastal Waterway runs 1,000 miles from Carrabelle, Florida to Brownsville, Texas [MM 682]. Distances on the Gulf Intracoastal are measured in statute miles east or west of Harvey Lock in New Orleans and shown as EHL or WHL. On our trip we entered the Gulf Intracoastal at the Mobile Bay Ship Channel, GIWW mile 134 EHL. We left the GIWW at 34 EHL to go to Lake Pontchartrain and New Orleans. When returning, we reentered the Gulf Intracoastal at 34 EHL and took it all the way to Carrabelle, 380 EHL. The Gulf Intracoastal Waterway runs between a series of barrier islands and the mainland, similar to the East Coast Intracoastal Waterway. The well-marked channel is dredged to 10 feet.

Mobile, Alabama to Biloxi, Mississippi

The trip from Mobile to Biloxi is 85 miles, the first 20 of these in Mobile Bay. We ran in the rain and in Mobile Bay had a beam sea that became a following sea when we turned west into the Gulf Intracoastal Waterway. The sea was fairly rough and for only the second time on the entire trip, we had a crewmember who was seasick.

We left Mobile at 8:30 A.M. and arrived at Biloxi at 1 P.M., 4.5 hours later. The rain stopped and the sun came out as we arrived in Biloxi. We stayed at the Point Cadet Marina, next to three casinos.

Biloxi, Mississippi

Biloxi, Mississippi is a casino town with at least 8 casinos and more being built. The Mississippi casino law stretches the riverboat casino law to the limit. The casino hotels in Biloxi have the hotel part built on land and the casino part built on a barge chained to the dock. The casino is floating, but there is no way it could move.

All the casinos have a number of restaurants plus entertainment, so this turned out to be an interesting place to dock. One of the casinos next to the marina is Casino Magic, the night we were there they had an excellent free comedy show.

Point Cadet Marina
    119 Beach Blvd.
    Biloxi, MS 39530-4710
    Phone: (228) 436-0312

Approach Depth	12'	Diesel Fuel	no
Dockside Depth	10'	Mechanical Repairs	no
Accepts Transients	yes	Ships Store	yes
Dockside Power	30,50,100	Showers	yes
Dockside Water	yes	Laundromat	yes
Gasoline	no	Restaurant	at casino

Biloxi, Mississippi to New Orleans, Louisiana

From Biloxi to New Orleans the distance is 106 miles, the first 71 miles of these on the Gulf Intracoastal Waterway. At mile 34 EHL you leave the GIWW and enter the Rigolets, a canal that joins Lake Borgne and Lake Pontchartrain. Once in Lake Pontchartrain, you go about 25 miles across the lake to get to the marina area, since in the New Orleans area, all the marinas are on Lake Pontchartrain, not on the Mississippi River.

The marina area is on the south shore about two miles east of the causeway that crosses the lake. Since we were planning to spend five days in New Orleans, we rented a car because it's about eight miles from the marina area to the French Quarter. We stayed at the Orleans Marina, which was large and had all the amenities.

Orleans Marina [Lake Pontchartrain]
  221 Lake Marina Avenue
  New Orleans, LA 70124
  Phone: (504) 288-2351

Approach Depth	9'	Diesel Fuel	no
Dockside Depth	12'	Mechanical Repairs	no
Accepts Transients	yes	Ships Store	yes
Dockside Power	30,50,100	Showers	yes
Dockside Water	yes	Laundromat	yes
Gasoline	no	Restaurant	nearby

New Orleans, Louisiana

Visiting New Orleans adds 340 miles to the overall trip, but I think it is well worth it if you haven't been there. The distance from the end of Mobile Bay to New Orleans is 170 miles, and since you have to come back to Mobile Bay to continue east on the main trip, the side trip to New Orleans becomes 340 miles total. I had been to New Orleans several times on business; however, my wife Jeri, son Scott, and daughter-in-law Bonnie, had never been there before. New Orleans is a unique place that blends French and American culture as in no other place.

Our first night in New Orleans we had dinner at Joe's Crab, within walking distance from the marina. This was the only restaurant I have ever been in that offered all five kinds of crab: Blue, Dungeness, Snow,

Stone, and Softshell.

The next day we went to the French Quarter, took the trolley tour of the city, had dinner at Antoines, and then did Bourbon Street.

The next day we had breakfast at Brennans, which is quite an experience. This is not a buffet, but rather a three-course, fixed-price breakfast where you can select from 5 or 6 choices for each course. Their signature dessert is Banana's Foster, which they invented.

During the next several days we took a ride on the *Delta Queen*, a full-size Mississippi paddlewheel boat; took a plantation tour; and had some other fine meals.

New Orleans was the end of the second leg of our trip; we planned to leave our boat there for three and a half months. Normally, when we leave our boat for some months, we have it pulled out of the water and stored on land because this is cheaper. However, there was no dry storage possible in New Orleans.

I made a deal with the Orleans Marina to leave my boat in its slip for 30 cents per foot instead of 1 dollar per foot, on the condition that I get my boat out of there before the Super Bowl. We flew home from New Orleans on October 7, 1996 and returned on January 17, 1997 to resume the trip.

New Orleans, Louisiana to Biloxi, Mississippi

We arrived back in New Orleans at 1 P.M. on January 17 to continue our journey. The next day we left at 9:30 A.M., headed for Biloxi.

We arrived at Biloxi at 2:00 P.M., but not without incident. Coming into Biloxi, I got confused as to where the channel was and we ran aground. The props were touching bottom, but the boat was floating. We were able to slowly back out, churning sand.

A man in a small boat showed us the way to the channel. Once in the channel, when we speeded up there was severe vibration, though the boat ran without vibration below 1,000 rpm. We went back to the Point Cadet Marina where we had stayed last fall. At the marina, we had a diver check our props. Though he was unable to remove them, he couldn't see any damage; this led us to believe we had bent shafts.

We had arrived in Biloxi on a Saturday, so we would have to wait until Monday to get into a shipyard to pull the boat out of the water. At the Point Cadet Marina, the boat that was docked next to us was owned by a man named Les Lala. He told us about Cavacevich Boatyard, and he showed up at 8 A.M. on Monday morning to call them to see if they could work on our boat immediately. They said they could take the boat, so we slowly cruised over to the boatyard at 1,000 rpm, which took an hour. Les drove over to the boatyard to see that we were taken care of. He even offered to let us stay in his house while the boat was being repaired. What a guy!

When the boat was pulled out of the water, it was found that both shafts were bent and both props were also. We rented an Enterprise car and checked into the Casino Grand Hotel (which Les also arranged).

The lesson I learned here was that when I first became confused as to where we were, I should have stopped and taken a fix. I also learned that in the future if I run aground, I should immediately shut the engines off and call for a tow, not try to plow my way out. The Cavacevich Boatyard did a fantastic job straightening both shafts and props and having our boat ready to go by 12:30 the next day. The bill I thought was reasonable, and our boat insurance picked up all but $300.

Biloxi, Mississippi to Pensacola, Florida

The trip from Biloxi to Pensacola is 97 miles on the Gulf Intracoastal; however, since we got such a late start at 12:30 P.M., we would not make it to Pensacola that day. By 5:30 P.M., as it was starting to get dark, we came upon a 50-foot motor yacht doing 10 knots in our direction. We talked on the radio and found that they were going to the Bear Point Marina, 30 miles west of Pensacola. We followed them to the marina, gassed up, had dinner on board, and went to bed early.

The next day we decided to skip Pensacola and go right to Destin where we were meeting our next crew and where we were also visiting friends. However, the data for the marina we had planned to stay at in Pensacola is as follows.

Seville Harbor
> 600 S. Barracks Street
> Pensacola, FL 32507
> Phone: (850) 432-9620
> www.marinamgmt.com
> e-mail: Carolyn@marinamgmt.com

Approach Depth	10'	Diesel Fuel	yes
Dockside Depth	9'	Mechanical Repairs	yes
Accepts Transients	yes	Ships Store	yes
Dockside Power	30,50	Showers	yes
Dockside Water	yes	Laundromat	yes
Gasoline	yes	Restaurant	nearby

Pensacola, Florida to Destin, Florida

The distance from Pensacola to Destin is only 30 miles; however, Destin is a very popular beach resort and a nice place to visit. We pulled into Sandestin's Baytowne Marina and called our friends Guy and Thea Woodluff, who owned a condo in Destin. We would spend the next several days with them and be joined by our next crew, who were Peter and Maria Doelp. I played golf with Guy in Destin, which was the only time I played golf on the entire boat trip. This tells you how much fun the boat trip was, since I normally play golf twice a week.

Sandestin's Baytowne Marina
    9300 Emerald Coast Parkway
    Sandestin, FL 32550
    Phone: (850) 267-7777
    www.sandestin.com
    e-mail: miller@sandestin.com

Approach Depth	7.5'	Diesel Fuel	yes
Dockside Depth	6'	Mechanical Repairs	yes
Accepts Transients	yes	Ships Store	yes
Dockside Power	30,50,100	Showers	yes
Dockside Water	yes	Laundromat	yes
Gasoline	yes	Restaurant	yes

Destin, Florida to Panama City, Florida

The distance from Destin to Panama City is only 45 miles, but there was a storm forecast for the afternoon, so we ran ahead of the storm and got there before 1:00 P.M. We watched the storm from a restaurant next to the Bay Point Marina. The Bay Point Marina is actually in Panama City Beach, on a barrier island on the other side of the Intracoastal Waterway from Panama City. However, you might consider staying in Panama City, which has many marinas and is the largest marine center on the Florida coast north of Tampa.

Bay Point Marina
    3824 Hatteras Land
    Panama City, FL 32408
    Phone: (850) 235-6911
    www.baypointmarina.net
    e-mail: sburt123@aol.com

Approach Depth	6'	Diesel Fuel	yes
Dockside Depth	6'	Mechanical Repairs	yes
Accepts Transients	yes	Ships Store	yes
Dockside Power	30,50,100	Showers	yes
Dockside Water	yes	Laundromat	yes
Gasoline	yes	Restaurant	yes

Panama City to Carrabelle, Florida

We had nice weather for the 80-mile trip from Panama City to Carrabelle. Cruising the Gulf Intracoastal Waterway is quite scenic and the channels are well marked. Carrabelle, at the eastern end of the Gulf Intracoastal Waterway, is a favorite jumping-off place to cross the Gulf to the west coast of Florida.

Carrabelle, Florida

Since the trip from Carrabelle to Cedar Keys is 120 miles straight across the Gulf and 180 miles to Tarpon Springs, it is prudent to wait for good weather before crossing. I have talked to people who had to wait as long as two weeks in Carrabelle before the weather was good enough for the crossing. The town is well equipped to service yachtsmen waiting to make the crossing.

Carrabelle was a place where we made another crew change, with Peter and Maria Doelp leaving and George and Helen Roth arriving. We were staying at the Moorings Marina, through whom we made arrangements for a driver to take the Doelps to the Tallahassee Airport and bring the Roths back. The crew switch was made on Super Bowl Sunday, 1997. We ate on the boat that night and watched Green Bay win the Super Bowl.

The Moorings Marina
 1000 Highway 98
 Carrabelle, FL 32322
 Phone: (850) 697-2800
 www.mooringscarrabelle.com
 e-mail: moorings@mooringscarrabelle.com

Approach Depth	15'	Diesel Fuel	yes
Dockside Depth	10'	Mechanical Repairs	yes
Accepts Transients	yes	Ships Store	yes
Dockside Power	30,50	Showers	yes
Dockside Water	yes	Laundromat	yes
Gasoline	yes	Restaurant	nearby

For this boat, with 120-mile range, the destination from Carrabelle should have been Suwannee River, where gas and diesel are available. Arrival at Suwannee should have been determined *before* leaving Carrabelle. Cedar Key would have been out of the plan; however, a crew change scheduled at this location made it necessary to get there.

These destinations are not recommended, because they are difficult to navigate even in perfect conditions. Anchoring in a navigation channel is very dangerous.

Many boaters cross the Gulf through the night, with arrival at Tampa Bay during daylight. Range should be a major factor to determine the boat to purchase for this trip. Grounding became a regular routine for this boat. Staying inside the markers is critical: look forward and backward, keeping the boat aligned inside the buoys or markers.

Carrabelle to Cedar Key

The trip from Carrabelle to Cedar Key is 120 miles and from Cedar Key to Tarpon Springs is 50 miles. There is no gas or diesel at Cedar Key, so you must have a range of 180 miles since you can't fill up until Tarpon Springs. Our boat had a range of only 120 miles, so we went to Suwannee River, which is only 105 miles from Carrabelle and has gas and diesel. However, you can only get into Suwannee River at high tide. We were lucky that we arrived at high tide. If I had it to do over again in the same boat, I would have carried an extra 100 gallons of gas aboard in plastic Jerry cans and skipped Suwannee River.

We expected to leave Carrabelle at 8:00 A.M.; however, the weather forecast was too windy to go straight across and the weather was supposed to get worse later in the week. The people at the Moorings Marina showed me a protected route that stayed within 10 miles of shore all the way across and therefore shielded us from the east winds. We finally left at 10:00 A.M. and the route turned out to be great. It was mildly rough for the first two hours, after which it got quite smooth.

When I originally planned this trip, we were going to go from Carrabelle to Suwannee River, and in fact that is what we did. We should have planned to go from Carrabelle to Cedar Key directly, because that's where we ended up that night. The story is an interesting one:

We arrived at the marina in Suwannee River at 5:00 P.M. The boat took 200 gallons, and since we only carry 240 gallons, we should have carried extra gas in Jerry cans to be safe. While we were gassing up, I mentioned to the man at the marina that the channel in the Suwannee River was very shallow at low tide, since our depth meter showed we were in 4 feet of water and our boat draws 37 inches. The man said that this was *high* tide, and the channel was only 1 foot deep at low tide.

We checked the tide chart and found that we would be stranded there until the following afternoon. We decided to leave immediately and try to get to Cedar Key, 16 miles south, before dark.

By the time we left, it was 6:00 P.M. and the channel was even shallower. I had to plane to raise the boat in the water. It is scary to plane at 18 miles per hour with 6 inches of water under the boat.

We made it out of the Suwannee River into the Gulf without running aground, but it was starting to get dark since it was January 27th. We ran the 11 miles to the Cedar Key Channel in the dark using GPS and following flashing buoys. From this point, we had to negotiate 5 miles of narrow channel to the Cedar Key Municipal dock.

We had four people on board and everyone had a job. George Roth was at the helm; Helen Roth held a flashlight on the depth meter, which was the only gauge whose light was burnt out; my wife, Jeri, used the handheld halogen light to spot channel markers; and I read the chart with a flashlight to identify channel markers and determine course headings.

After successfully negotiating 4 miles of channel, at 8:00 P.M. we ran aground. We checked the tide chart we had gotten in Suwannee River and saw that low tide was at 10:00 P.M. and the next high tide was at 4:00 A.M. We turned the generator on and then the lights and air conditioning.

We had a nice dinner with wine, after which we went to bed around 10:00 P.M. We set the alarm for 2:00 A.M. because we thought we would be floating by then. I got a very accurate fix with the GPS so I would know which way to move the boat once we were floating.

At 2:00 A.M. Jeri got everyone up because we were floating. We moved the boat about 50 feet into the center of the channel and dropped anchor. We were now in 10 feet of water and we went back to bed.

Street musicians in New Orleans

New Orleans

Props and shafts being straightened in Biloxi

Cedar Key
to Key West

West Coast of Florida

CHAPTER 12

CEDAR KEY TO KEY WEST
WEST COAST OF FLORIDA

DESTINATION	MARINA	STATUTE MILES	CUMULATIVE MILES
(Depart Cedar Key)			
Tarpon Springs, FL	Port Tarpon Marina	60	3558
St. Petersburg, FL			
Longboat Key, FL	Longboat Key Moorings	65	3623
Boca Grande, FL	Millers Marina	43	3666
Marco Island, FL	Marco River Marina	65	3731
Key West, FL	The Galleon Marina	98	3829

Charts Required:
> *Maptech ChartKit—Florida West Coast and The Keys*

Cruising Guide:
> *Waterway Guide—Southern*

The destinations where the author stayed, shown in bold type, are described in the following chapter. The other destinations are listed as intermediate ports if a shorter cruising day is desired. Check the cruising guide for more information.

Cedar Key to Tarpon Springs, Florida

We got up with the sunrise at 7:00 A.M.; we still had 8 feet of water under the boat and it was a beautiful blue-sky day. We left at 8:00 A.M. and followed a boat in the channel out to the Gulf. There wasn't much wind and the ride was very smooth.

We ran down the coast to Tarpon Springs, arriving there at 12:00 noon. We saw a number of dolphins on our way and it was very relaxing—quite a contrast to the previous day, which was exciting but certainly not relaxing.

Tarpon Springs, Florida

Tarpon Springs is the northern end of the Gulf Intracoastal on the west coast of Florida. From Tarpon Springs to Marco Island you have the choice of going inside or outside.

Tarpon Springs happens to be the sponge capital of the USA. The original sponge divers who settled here were Greek, so the town has a Greek flavor and a number of Greek restaurants. We visited the Sponge Diving Museum, saw the sponge and shrimp fleets, and had dinner at Poppas Greek Restaurant. We stayed at Port Tarpon Marina, which also had a nice restaurant where we had lunch.

Port Tarpon Marina [in Anclote River]

531 Anclote Road
Tarpon Springs, FL 34689
Phone: (727) 937-2200
www.porttarponmarina.com
e-Mail: brooke@porttarponmarina.com

Approach Depth	9'	Diesel Fuel	yes
Dockside Depth	9'	Mechanical Repairs	yes

Accepts Transients	yes	Ships Store	yes
Dockside Power	30,50	Showers	yes
Dockside Water	yes	Laundromat	no
Gasoline	yes	Restaurant	yes

Tarpon Springs to Longboat Key, Florida

We had originally planned to go on the inside to Longboat Key; however, because of the nice weather we changed our mind and ran on the outside. At Longboat Inlet, we went inside and promptly ran aground. The Gulf Intracoastal on the west coast of Florida is quite shallow, and you can run aground if you get slightly out of the channel.

Having learned my lesson in Biloxi, this time I called SeaTow. They pulled us off; the bill was $480, since the charge is based on the size of your boat.

We continued on the inside to our marina, the Longboat Key Moorings. This four-star facility had swimming, tennis, an 18-hole golf course, and an excellent restaurant in the marina. Longboat Key is a barrier island beach resort off of Sarasota, Florida. This is a nice place to stay for a few days, since it offers the cultural activities of Sarasota.

Longboat Key Mooring Marina
 2600 Harborside Drive
 Longboat Key, FL 34228
 Phone: (941) 383-8383 also (800) 858-0836
 www.longboatkeymarina.com

Approach Depth	7'	Diesel Fuel	yes
Dockside Depth	20'	Mechanical Repairs	no
Accepts Transients	yes	Ships Store	yes
Dockside Power	30,50,100	Showers	yes
Dockside Water	yes	Laundromat	yes
Gasoline	yes	Restaurant	yes

Longboat Key to Boca Grande, Florida

Our plan was to go inside to Venice Inlet and then go outside to Boca Grande. When we got to Venice Inlet we went outside, but it was very rough so we turned around and came back inside. We turned south on the Intracoastal, and within an hour we had run aground again.

We called SeaTow, and this time it cost $430. The reason the charge was less than the previous day is that we had a different SeaTow franchise and apparently they each figure up the bill a little differently. I had learned my lesson, so the next day I called Boat/U.S., and for $88, bought unlimited towing insurance for a whole year. Since we now had towing insurance, we would run aground only one more time on the entire trip.

We arrived at Boca Grande Marina (formerly Miller's) at 5:00 P.M.

Boca Grande Marina
224 Harbor Drive
Boca Grande, FL 33921
Phone: (941) 964-2100
www.bocagrandemarina.com

Approach Depth	8'	Diesel Fuel	yes
Dockside Depth	8'	Mechanical Repairs	yes
Accepts Transients	yes	Ships Store	yes
Dockside Power	30,50	Showers	yes
Dockside Water	yes	Laundromat	yes
Gasoline	yes	Restaurant	yes

Boca Grande, Florida

Boca Grande is the only town on Gasparilla Island, north of Captiva on Florida's west coast. This delightful island, about 7 miles long, has a maximum population of only about 3,500 in high season (February through April). The island has a very relaxed atmosphere, uncrowded beaches, great fishing, and a number of nice restaurants. The island is also noted for its bridge toll, which was $3.25 to get onto the island [now $4.00], though it is free to get off.

At the southern end of the island is Boca Grande Pass, world famous for tarpon fishing in May and June. Fishermen come from all over the world to catch the hard-fighting tarpon that can weigh several hundred pounds.

We stayed on Boca Grande for five days, since our friends George and Ann Lyons own a condo there. On one of those days, we rented a 19-foot outboard and cruised around the many small islands around Boca Grande. We saw many dolphins plus White Pelican Island, a sandbar with several hundred all-white pelicans. We went to Pine Island and had lunch at Bootleggers.

Another day we rented a golf cart that holds four people and toured the island.

Boca Grande to Marco Island

We switched crews again at Boca Grande as our friends George and Helen Roth left and our eldest son, Bick, and our daughter-in-law, Kathy, joined us.

We had originally planned to go to Captiva for one night and then onto Marco Island, from whence we would make our 98-mile crossing to Key West. But the weather forecast called for a front to come through, with some storm activity the following night. Consequently, we decided to skip Captiva and go right to Marco Island and make the crossing to Key West the next day, ahead of the storm.

We ran from Boca Grande to Marco Island in the Gulf; the water was flat, the sun was shining, and we had a beautiful ride. We stayed at the Marco River Marina, within walking distance of a number of restaurants.

Marco River Marina
    951 Bald Eagle Drive
    Marco Island, FL 34145
    Phone: (239) 394-2502
    www.marcoriver.com

Approach Depth	6'	Diesel Fuel	yes
Dockside Depth	6'	Mechanical Repairs	yes
Accepts Transients	yes	Ships Store	yes
Dockside Power	30,50	Showers	yes
Dockside Water	yes	Laundromat	no
Gasoline	yes	Restaurant	nearby

Marco Island to Key West

We left Marco Island at 8:30 A.M. and arrived in Key West at 2:15 P.M. We had flat seas but ran through two rainsqualls, each lasting about 30 minutes; though we heard some thunder, we didn't see any lightning.

Key West

We really enjoyed Key West, so we ended up staying there seven days. There are numerous shops, restaurants, and a lot of entertainment available in Key West.

We took the bus tour of the island, had lunch at a sidewalk cafe called Mango's, and visited Hemingway's house. Another day, my son, Bick, and I rented scooters and toured the entire island. There are a number of museums in Key West; one of the more interesting was Mel Fisher's Shipwreck Museum. One night we took a sunset cruise on a large sailboat. We had a number of good meals; however, the best was at Louie's Back Yard, which is open-air on the Gulf.

The Galleon Marina is the best place to stay because it is in the old town and is within walking distance to everything. This was the most expensive marina that we stayed at on the entire trip ($2.25 per foot per day); however, it has all the amenities: swimming pool, sandy beach, and so forth.

It is interesting to note that Key West was the southernmost point on our trip, whereas Mackinac Island was the northernmost point. These two islands are both very interesting places to visit; however, they couldn't be more different.

Galleon Marina
619 Front Street
Key West, FL 33040
Phone: (305) 292-1292
www.galleonresort.com

Approach Depth	6'	Diesel Fuel	yes
Dockside Depth	6'	Mechanical Repairs	yes
Accepts Transients	yes	Ships Store	yes
Dockside Power	30,50	Showers	yes
Dockside Water	yes	Laundromat	no
Gasoline	yes	Restaurant	nearby

Nittany Navy in Gulf Intracoastal Waterway

Tarpon Springs, Florida—The Sponge Capital

The beach at Boca Grande, Florida

The Galleon Marina at Key West

Key West to West Palm Beach

Intracoastal Waterway

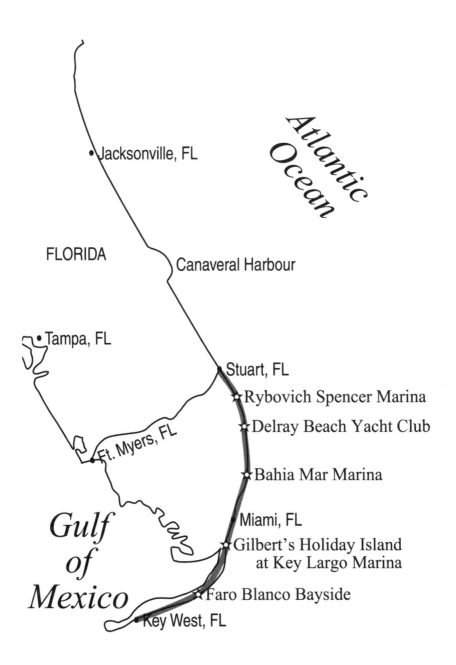

CHAPTER 13

KEY WEST TO WEST PALM BEACH
INTRACOASTAL WATERWAY

DESTINATION	MARINA	STATUTE MILES	CUMULATIVE MILES
(Depart Key West)			
Marathon, FL	Faro Blanco Bayside	50	3879
Key Largo, FL	Gilbert's Holiday Island	59	3938
Fort Lauderdale, FL	Bahia Mar Marina	50	3988
Delray Beach, FL	Delray Beach Yacht Club	25	4013
West Palm Beach, FL	Rybovich Spencer	20	4033

Charts Required:

Maptech ChartKit—Florida West Coast and The Keys

Cruising Guide:

Waterway Guide—Southern

Key West to Marathon

Our friends Jim and Betty Ann McArdle joined us in Key West for the cruise through the Keys.

From Key West to Marathon is approximately 50 statute miles, with the most direct route being the Hawk Channel. The Hawk Channel runs along the Gulf side of the Keys between the islands and outer reefs, which make the channel smoother than the Gulf itself but not as smooth as taking the inside route. The inside route to Marathon has shallow water and is longer.

We had planned to leave Key West for Marathon via the Hawk Channel on Tuesday, February 11, 1997; however, it was windy and the Coast Guard had posted small craft warnings. We decided to stay another day in Key West, which was a good decision since the next day the winds had died down and the weather was beautiful.

Our route to Marathon would follow the Hawk Channel for about 40 miles, at which point we would go inside 10 miles south of Marathon. The last 10 miles would be on the ICW; after that we would stay on the ICW all the way to New Jersey.

Marathon

Marathon is actually the city located on the island of Vaca Key; however, it is common for people to refer to the entire island as Marathon. The island has a population of around 8,000 and has a hospital and an airport. Marathon also has many good restaurants, plus quite a few motels and hotels.

We stayed at the Faro Blanco Bayside Marina, known for its landmark lighthouse located next to the docks. This marina has a very nice swimming pool facility and an excellent restaurant.

Faro Blanco Bayside Marina [MM 1193.2]
  1996 Overseas Highway
  Marathon, FL 33050
  Phone: (305) 743-9018
  www.spottswood.com/html/blanco/marina.htm

Approach Depth	7'	Diesel Fuel	yes
Dockside Depth	7'	Mechanical Repairs	no
Accepts Transients	yes	Ships Store	yes
Dockside Power	30,50	Showers	yes
Dockside Water	yes	Laundromat	yes
Gasoline	yes	Restaurant	yes

Marathon to Key Largo

The trip from Marathon to Key Largo is 59 miles following the ICW in Florida Bay. We left Marathon at 8:30 A.M. and arrived in Key Largo at 2:00 P.M.

Key Largo

Key Largo is 30 miles long and is home to the famous Ocean Reef Club. We stayed at Gilbert's Holiday Island at Key Largo Marina, located on the ICW at the US Route 1 Bridge where US 1 crosses over from mainland Florida to the Keys. This marina is small but is very convenient to both the ICW and US 1. The marina has a small swimming pool and a tiki bar.

We took a cab to the Sundowners Restaurant in Key Largo, where we had a good meal.

Gilbert's Holiday Island at Key Largo Marina
107900 Overseas Highway
Key Largo, FL 33037
Phone: (305) 451-1133, also (800) 274-6701

Approach Depth	10'	Diesel Fuel	yes
Dockside Depth	8'	Mechanical Repairs	no
Accepts Transients	yes	Ships Store	no
Dockside Power	30,50	Showers	yes
Dockside Water	yes	Laundromat	yes
Gasoline	yes	Restaurant	yes

Key Largo to Ft. Lauderdale

Our original plan was to go from Key Largo to Miami; however, we were there during the week of the Miami boat show and there were no slips available in Miami. We were able to get a slip in Ft. Lauderdale, so as a result we never got to stay in Miami on our boat; nevertheless, I have included a paragraph on Miami in this chapter.

You will recall that just before we arrived at Key Largo we had to switch to individual chart #14F instead of simply switching to the next chart kit. This is because there are 30 miles missing between the two chart kits. Individual Chart #14F includes this missing section, which is between SM 1140 and SM 1110 on the ICW. Therefore, when you leave Key Largo, you are using individual Chart #14F up to SM 1110. At this point, you switch to Chart Kit—Jacksonville to Miami, Chart #27. SM 1110 is not shown but is at the bottom of the chart. Follow the magenta line on Charts 27 and 28 through Biscayne Bay to Miami. Chart 30 is where the marinas are for Miami and Miami Beach. Going north on the ICW, Chart 29 comes after Chart 30 and the next chart after that is Chart 33. Our marina in Ft. Lauderdale was at SM 1064.5.

ChartKit—Jacksonville to Miami is no longer available. Intracoastal charts for the east coast of Florida are: 11467, 11472, 11485, and 11489.

The trip from Miami to Ft. Lauderdale is very slow, much of it no-wake zone. There are also many bridges, including 4 or 5 that we couldn't get under but had to wait until they opened. The good news is that although the trip is very slow here, the houses on either side of the waterway are so spectacular you want to slow down just to enjoy them.

Miami

Had we been able to stay in Miami, we planned to stay at the Miami Beach Marina, which is a very large, 400-slip marina with every amenity nearby. Miami Beach is, of course, a large resort offering every type of entertainment, the best shopping, excellent restaurants, and so forth. The Miami Beach Marina is located on the main channel on the southern tip of the Miami Beach Island very close to the Ocean [Chart 30].

Ft. Lauderdale

Ft. Lauderdale is virtually a city of canals. You can go to stores and restaurants by boat. We stayed at the large Bahia Mar Marina, which is beautifully located on the ICW right next to the beach and the Raddison Hotel. There are several good restaurants in the hotel and several others within walking distance. This is a great place to stay if you would like to spend several days on the beach.

Bahia Mar Marina
> Raddison Yachting Center
> 801 Seabreeze Boulevard
> Fort Lauderdale, FL 33316
> Phone: (954) 764-2233
> www.bahiamarhotel.com/yachting.htm

Approach Depth	12'	Diesel Fuel	yes
Dockside Depth	10'	Mechanical Repairs	no
Accepts Transients	yes	Ships Store	yes
Dockside Power	30,50,100	Showers	yes
Dockside Water	yes	Laundromat	yes
Gasoline	yes	Restaurant	yes

Ft. Lauderdale to Delray Beach

The trip from Ft. Lauderdale to Delray Beach is only 25 miles; however, it took us 3 hours because much of the way is "no wake" or "minimum wake," plus the many bridge openings. We were lucky: with our boat's 15-foot 9-inch clearance, we were able to sneak under three 15-foot bridges at low tide. The bridge gauges were reading 16 feet 5 inches at the time.

As with the trip from Miami to Ft. Lauderdale, this trip is also full of beautiful homes and beautiful boats on the waterway. It makes you wonder how so many people have that much money.

We stayed at the Delray Beach Yacht Club [SM 1039] because it was close to Boca Raton where my mother spends the winters. Our friends Jim and Betty Ann McArdle flew home, and we stayed with my mother for a week. Had we not been visiting my mother, we would have skipped Delray Beach and gone directly from Ft. Lauderdale to West Palm Beach.

Delray Beach Yacht Club [MM 1039.9]
110 Macfarlane Drive
Delray Beach, FL 33483
Phone: (407) 272-2700

Approach Depth	8'	Diesel Fuel	no
Dockside Depth	6'	Mechanical Repairs	no
Accepts Transients	yes	Ships Store	no
Dockside Power	30,50	Showers	yes
Dockside Water	yes	Laundromat	yes
Gasoline	no	Restaurant	no

Delray Beach to West Palm Beach

The distance from Delray Beach to West Palm Beach is only 20 miles. The reason most people would go to Palm Beach is that it is a nice resort and a good place to visit. We went there because it has a large airport (West Palm Beach Airport) and a number of boatyards where we could leave our boat for four months. Therefore, West Palm Beach was a convenient place for us to end the third leg of our trip and fly home.

We left our boat at the Rybovich-Spencer Boatyard [SM 1019] and flew home on February 20, 1997.

Rybovich-Spencer Marina [MM 1020.0]
4200 N. Flagler Drive
West Palm Beach, FL 33407
Phone: (561) 844-1800

Approach Depth	9'	Diesel Fuel	yes
Dockside Depth	8'	Mechanical Repairs	yes
Accepts Transients	yes	Ships Store	yes
Dockside Power	30,50,100	Showers	yes
Dockside Water	yes	Laundromat	no
Gasoline	yes	Restaurant	no

Approaching Miami from Biscayne Bay

The ICW in Fort Lauderdale, Florida

West Palm Beach
to Savannah

Intracoastal Waterway

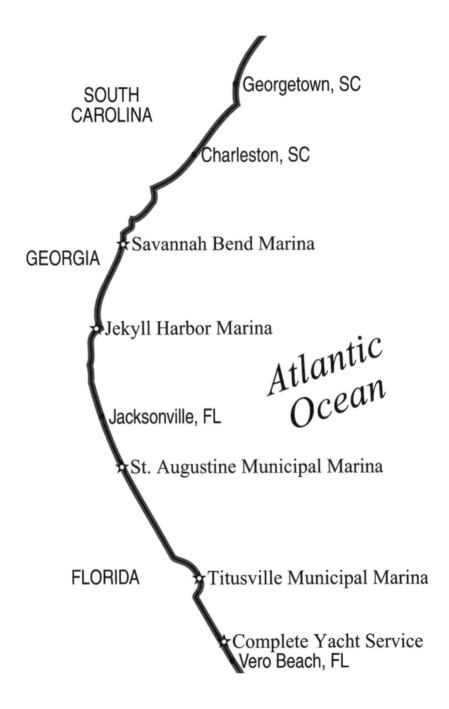

SOUTH
CAROLINA

Georgetown, SC

Charleston, SC

☆Savannah Bend Marina

GEORGIA

☆Jekyll Harbor Marina

*Atlantic
Ocean*

Jacksonville, FL

☆St. Augustine Municipal Marina

FLORIDA

☆Titusville Municipal Marina

☆Complete Yacht Service
Vero Beach, FL

CHAPTER 14

WEST PALM BEACH TO SAVANNAH
INTRACOASTAL WATERWAY

DESTINATION	MARINA	STATUTE MILES	CUMULATIVE MILES
(Depart West Palm Beach)			
Vero Beach, FL	Complete Yacht Service	68	4101
Titusville, FL	Titusville Municipal Marina	74	4175
Daytona Beach, FL			
St. Augustine, FL	St. Augustine Municipal	100	4275
Jacksonville Beach, FL			
Jekyll Island, GA	Jekyll Harbor Marina	94	4369
Catherines Sound Area, GA			
Savannah, GA	Savannah Bend Marina	102	4471

Charts Required:

NOAA Charts 11467, 11472, 11485, 11489

Maptech ChartKit—Norfolk to Jacksonville via ICW

Cruising Guide:

Waterway Guide—Southern

Waterway Guide—Mid-Atlantic

(On the preceding page, the destinations where the author stayed are shown in bold type. These destinations are described in the following chapter. The other destinations are listed as intermediate ports if a shorter cruising day is desired. Check the cruising guide for information on intermediate ports.)

West Palm Beach to Vero Beach

The trip from Palm Beach to Vero Beach on the ICW is 58 miles.

We flew from Philadelphia to West Palm Beach on May 13, 1997 to begin the fourth and final leg of the Great Circle Cruise. Our plan was to go to Vero Beach the next day and pick up Gene and Mildred Winne, who would go with us to St. Augustine.

We went to Vero Beach on the 14th, and on the 15th we headed north with the Winnes on board. At approximately 11:00 A.M., our port engine suddenly lost rpm and shut down. The nearest marina was three miles back, so we turned around and went there on one engine.

A mechanic checked our engine and told us that it had blown a rod through the bottom of the block, split the oil pan, and dumped the oil into the bilge, after which the engine froze. We had traveled 4,000 miles without any engine problems; however, this made up for it, since the engine was totaled. The engine was a 454 cubic inch, 350 Hp, V8 inboard with 1,150 hours on it. We made arrangements with the Complete Yacht Services Marina, in Vero Beach, to get a new engine and flew home.

On June 19th Jeri and I flew back to West Palm Beach, rented a car, and drove back to Vero Beach to resume the boat trip. The people who had planned to go with us on this portion of the trip could not make it on the revised schedule, so Jeri and I would take the boat ourselves from Vero Beach to Baltimore. Our son, Chris, and his wife, Claudine, would join us there for the completion of our trip back to Avalon, New Jersey.

Complete Marine Service (MM 951.7)
2915 Aviation Boulevard
Vero Beach, FL 32960
Phone: (772) 778-2300

Approach Depth	6'	Diesel Fuel	yes
Dockside Depth	6'	Mechanical Repairs	yes
Accepts Transients	yes	Ships Store	yes
Dockside Power	30,50	Showers	yes
Dockside Water	yes	Laundromat	yes
Gasoline	yes	Restaurant	no

Vero Beach to Titusville

On June 21, 1997 we resumed our trip with one new engine and one old engine. We did the 74 miles from Vero Beach to Titusville in 5 hours. We had to hold the engine rpm down to 3,000 because we were breaking in the new engine. Since we normally cruise between 3,300 and 3,500 it took us a little longer than normal to make our destination.

Using the *Maptech ChartKit Norfolk to Jacksonville via ICW,* follow Charts 42, 43, 47, and 48 to Titusville. The Titusville Municipal Marina is at SM 878 just north of the Titusville swing bridge.

NOTE: The Titusville Swing Bridge (vertical clearance 9 feet) closes Monday through Friday 6:15 to 7:15 A.M. and 3 to 4:30 P.M.

Titusville

Titusville is the closest town to the Kennedy Space Center. If you have not visited the Kennedy Space Center, it is well worth your while to spend a day there. You can make arrangements at the marina to get transportation to the Space Center. Once there, a bus system transports you around from the visitor center complex to the space shuttle launch site, the manned space exhibit, and the space station exhibit. Everything there is very well done. However, the manned space exhibit, which features the Apollo Moon Program, is worth the trip all by itself.

After visiting the Space Center, a great place to have dinner in Titusville is the Dixie Crossroads Restaurant, which features rock shrimp. This type of shrimp comes in a very hard shell that requires a machine to split. This restaurant has invented that machine, and when you order, you get several dozen shrimp with their shells split open and swimming in butter.

Titusville Municipal Marina
451 Marina Road
Titusville, FL 32796
Phone: (321) 383-5600

Approach Depth	8'	Diesel Fuel	yes
Dockside Depth	8'	Mechanical Repairs	no
Accepts Transients	yes	Ships Store	yes
Dockside Power	30,50	Showers	yes
Dockside Water	yes	Laundromat	yes
Gasoline	yes	Restaurant	yes

Titusville to St. Augustine

The trip from Titusville to St. Augustine is 100 miles on the ICW, starting at SM 878 at the Titusville Marina and ending at SM 778 at the St. Augustine Municipal Marina.

Most of the ICW goes through wetlands between the mainland and barrier islands. This section is typical of this beautiful terrain, with many types of water birds such as egrets, herons, pelicans, wild ducks, seagulls, and such. The trip took seven hours, in part because of a number of no-wake areas; however, the scenery was so beautiful that the seven hours went quickly.

St. Augustine

St. Augustine, founded in 1565, is the oldest permanent European settlement in the United States. The St. Augustine Municipal Marina is located in the heart of the old city, within walking distance to almost everything. The fort, which has a moat, is only a 5-minute walk from the marina. Construction on the fort started in 1672.

Across the street from the marina is the A1A Brewery, a microbrewery and restaurant. The food here is quite good and very unusual, since they serve no red meat. If you go there, try the cheese ale soup; it is excellent.

We stayed in St. Augustine for three days and had a wonderful time. I would recommend the trolley tour, the movie at the tourist center, and the Lightner Museum, along with the fort and just walking around the old town.

St. Augustine Municipal Marina
111 Avenida Menendez
St. Augustine, FL 32084
Phone: (904) 825-1026
www.ci.st-augustine.fl.us

Approach Depth	16'	Diesel Fuel	yes
Dockside Depth	16'	Mechanical Repairs	no
Accepts Transients	yes	Ships Store	yes
Dockside Power	30,50	Showers	yes
Dockside Water	yes	Laundromat	yes
Gasoline	yes	Restaurant	yes

St. Augustine to Jekyll Island

St. Augustine to Jekyll Island is 94 miles on the ICW; we made the trip in 6 hours and 45 minutes. The Jekyll Harbor Marina is at SM 684.

Jekyll Island

Jekyll Island was purchased in 1886 by a group of America's richest families as a private resort. The Rockefellers, Morgans, and Vanderbilts all vacationed here. The state of Georgia purchased the island from the exclusive Jekyll Island Club in 1947. The island today is an elegant resort with a number of hotels and 63 holes of golf. One of the island attractions is a tour of the mansion-size "cottages" from the Jekyll Island Club era.

Jekyll Harbor Marina
1 Harbor Road
Jekyll Island, GA 31527
Phone: (912) 635-3137
www.jekyllharbor.com

Approach Depth	12'	Diesel Fuel	yes
Dockside Depth	10'	Mechanical Repairs	no
Accepts Transients	yes	Ships Store	yes
Dockside Power	30,50	Showers	yes
Dockside Water	yes	Laundromat	yes
Gasoline	yes	Restaurant	yes

Jekyll Island to Savannah

Jekyll Island to Savannah is 102 miles; we made the trip in 5.5 hours using the *Chart Kit—Norfolk to Jacksonville*. The ICW only comes within 6 or 7 miles of downtown Savannah, so this marina is as convenient as any. At the time we were there, there were no marinas in downtown Savannah. We spent two days there and we took a cab into the city each day.

Savannah, Georgia

Neither Jeri nor I had ever been to Savannah before, so we were surprised by how much of its original character this city retains. Savannah is a small city by today's standards; however, it is built around 21 squares that look as if they haven't changed since before the Civil War. The squares are basically small city parks with gardens surrounded by old, elegant homes. The best way to see the squares is to take a trolley tour.

Savannah also has a number of good restaurants. One in particular that we can recommend is the Pink House. Savannah is also noted for its waterfront area located on the Savannah River. This area has been restored with interesting shops, restaurants, and Irish pubs. There are a number of Irish pubs that also have authentic Irish music. We were told that thousands of people come to Savannah every year for Saint Patrick's Day.

Savannah Bend Marina (MM 582.3)
Route 14, Box 188
Old Tybee Road
Savannah, GA
Phone: (912) 897-3625

Approach Depth	8'	Diesel Fuel	yes
Dockside Depth	6'	Mechanical Repairs	yes
Accepts Transients	yes	Ships Store	no
Dockside Power	30,50	Showers	yes
Dockside Water	yes	Laundromat	yes
Gasoline	yes	Restaurant	no

171

The Fort at St. Augustine, Florida

A house on one of the beautiful squares in Savannah

SAVANNAH TO NORFOLK

INTRACOASTAL WATERWAY

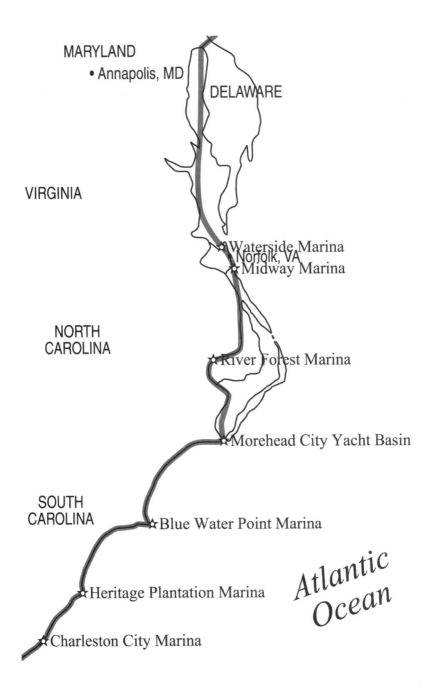

Chapter 15

Savannah to Norfolk
Intracoastal Waterway

Destination	Marina	Statute Miles	Cumulative Miles
(Depart Savannah)			
Charleston, SC	Charleston City Marina	113	4584
Georgetown, SC	Heritage Plantation Marina	74	4658
Southport, NC	Blue Water Point Marina	75	4733
Wrightsville Beach, NC			
Morehead, City, NC	Morehead City Yacht Basin	116	4849
Belhaven, NC	River Forest Marina	68	4917
Coinjock, NC	Midway Marina	87	5004
Norfolk, VA	Waterside Marina	49	5053

Charts Required:

Maptech ChartKit—Norfolk, VA to Jacksonville, FL

Cruising Guide:

Waterway Guide—Mid-Atlantic

(On the preceding page, the destinations where the author stayed are shown in bold type. These destinations are described in the following chapter. The other destinations are listed as intermediate ports if a shorter cruising day is desired. Check the cruising guide for information on intermediate ports.)

Savannah to Charleston

We did the entire 113-mile trip from Savannah to Charleston in 6.5 hours. We did not stop in Beaufort; however, it looked like a nice town, and had we had more time, we would have stayed there. Use *Maptech Chart Kit—Norfolk to Jacksonville*. This entire trip is pretty much through wetlands and is quite beautiful.

We stayed at the Charleston City Marina, which is new and very nice. This marina has a great location since the tour buses stop there, the water tour boats dock there, and there are several restaurants, including Pussers, which is very good.

Charleston, SC

Charleston was founded in 1670 by the British. By the time George Washington was president, Charleston was the fourth largest city in the United States, with only Philadelphia, New York, and Boston being larger. During pre-Civil War days, wealthy plantation owners would build houses in Charleston to escape the summer heat inland. The unique architecture of these Charleston homes was designed to catch the maximum amount of sea breeze by having a side porch that the wind could pass through instead of a front porch that would block the wind. These houses often had a fake front door, since the real door was off of the side porch.

We would recommend a bus tour of the historic district, including some of the elegant homes. The visitors' center has a movie of the history of Charleston, which is worthwhile. They have boat tours to Fort Sumter, the shelling of which marked the beginning of the Civil War. Charleston is also known for its wonderful restaurants, including the South Bend Brewery and Hymans Seafood. Hymans Seafood Restaurant is really outstanding; it deserves the line of people on the sidewalk outside waiting to get in.

Charleston City Marina (MM 469.5)
> 17 Lockwood Drive
> Charleston, SC 29401
> Phone: (803) 723-5098
> www.charlestoncitymarina.com

Approach Depth	10'	Diesel Fuel	no
Dockside Depth	10'	Mechanical Repairs	no
Accepts Transients	yes	Ships Store	yes
Dockside Power	30,50	Showers	yes
Dockside Water	yes	Laundromat	yes
Gasoline	no	Restaurant	yes

Charleston to Georgetown, SC

The trip from Charleston to Georgetown is 66 miles; however, we went another 8 miles to stay at the Heritage Plantation Marina because our friends Jim and Carol Davies lived near there. The Heritage Plantation also includes a beautiful 18-hole golf course, which is open to the public. This would be a good place to stay if you want to play golf; otherwise you might want to stay at a marina in Georgetown.

Heritage Plantation Marina (MM 394.0)
1823 Heritage Drive
Pawleys Island, SC 29585
Phone: (843) 237-3650
www.heritageplantation.com

Approach Depth	30'	Diesel Fuel	no
Dockside Depth	30'	Mechanical Repairs	no
Accepts Transients	yes	Ships Store	no
Dockside Power	30,50	Showers	yes
Dockside Water	yes	Laundromat	yes
Gasoline	no	Restaurant	no

Georgetown to Southport

From Georgetown to Southport, the ICW winds through the wetlands between barrier islands and the mainland. The trip is 75 miles; there are a number of slow areas and many bridges that require opening.

We left Georgetown at 8:15 A.M. and arrived at our marina near Southport at 2:15 P.M. We stayed at the Blue Water Point Marina, next to the beach. We had dinner at the Fish House Restaurant, in the marina.

Blue Water Point Marina
West Beach Drive to 57th Place
Oak Island, NC 28465
Phone: (910) 278-1230
www.bluewaterpointmotel.com/html/marina.html

Approach Depth	5'	Diesel Fuel	yes
Dockside Depth	5'	Mechanical Repairs	no
Accepts Transients	yes	Ships Store	yes
Dockside Power	30,50	Showers	yes

Dockside Water	yes	Laundromat	no
Gasoline	yes	Restaurant	yes

Southport to Morehead City

We did the 116-mile trip from Southport to Morehead City in 8 hours. We did not stay in Wrightsville Beach but chose to go all the way to Morehead City. We left at 7:10 a.m. and arrived at 3:15 p.m. We had to wait for three bridge openings and the worst was a pontoon bridge where we waited 40 minutes. We stayed at the Morehead City Yacht Basin Marina (SM 204).

Morehead City

We stayed in Morehead City because we have several friends who own condos in Atlantic Beach, which is across the bridge from Morehead City. We stayed with one of them while we were there. You can choose to stay in Morehead City or Beaufort, which is right next to Morehead City and both towns are on the ICW. If you choose Beaufort, the marinas are in the waterfront area, which has many nice shops and restaurants within walking distance. If you stay in Morehead City, you might want to rent a car to visit Fort Macon, which is on the north end of Bogue Bank Island and was used in the civil war. Also, if you had a car, you could go to the beach at Atlantic Beach and visit Beaufort.

Morehead City Yacht Basin Marina (MM 203.5)
    208 Arendell Street
    Morehead City, NC 28570
    Phone: (252) 726-6862
    www.moreheadcityyachtbasin.com

Approach Depth	12'	Diesel Fuel	yes
Dockside Depth	8'	Mechanical Repairs	yes
Accepts Transients	yes	Ships Store	yes
Dockside Power	30,50	Showers	yes
Dockside Water	yes	Laundromat	yes
Gasoline	yes	Restaurant	yes

Morehead City to Belhaven

All the way from Miami, the ICW runs very close to the Atlantic Ocean. However, at Morehead City, the ICW goes inland via canal to the Neuse River. The ICW then follows the Western Shore of Pamlico Sound to the Pungo River to Belhaven. Whereas Morehead City was a few miles from the Beach, Belhaven is about 60 miles east of the Beach, which is now on Hatteras Island on the southern end of the Outer Banks.

We stayed at the River Forest Marina in Belhaven, which is a B&B in an old southern mansion with pillars. They have a restaurant there which features a buffet. They also have a nice bar and a swimming pool. The day we stayed there was July 4, 1997, and we watched the fireworks from our boat. This was the second Fourth of July that we spent on our boat trip. July 4, 1996, we were on Mackinac Island, MI.

River Forest Marina (MM 135.0)
738 E. Main Street
Belhaven, NC 27810
Phone: (252) 943-2151
www.riverforestmarina.com

Approach Depth	10'	Diesel Fuel	yes
Dockside Depth	10'	Mechanical Repairs	yes
Accepts Transients	yes	Ships Store	yes
Dockside Power	30,50	Showers	yes

| Dockside Water | yes | Laundromat | yes |
| Gasoline | yes | Restaurant | yes |

Belhaven to Coinjock

The trip from Belhaven to Coinjock is 87 miles long. There are two routes across the Sound. One course takes you to the Dismal Swamp Canal and the other course goes to the Virginia Cut Canal. The Virginia Cut Canal is the primary ICW route. The Dismal Swamp Canal is shorter in miles but is known for floating debris. Both canal routes come together south of Norfolk. We chose the Virginia Cut route, which goes to Coinjock.

The Albemarle Sound has a reputation for being the roughest piece of water on the ICW. The reason for this is that it is shallow and is protected from the Atlantic Ocean only by the Outer Banks, which are only sandbars. Winds coming from the ocean can whip up 6-ft. waves on the Sound, and due to the shallow water the waves are very close together. This condition can pound a boat severely. My recommendation when crossing the Albemarle Sound is to wait for a good weather forecast. When we crossed the Sound we had only 3-foot waves; however, it was pretty rough. We stayed at the Midway Marina, which does not have a restaurant; however, they lent us a car so we could drive to one.

About 30 minutes out of Belhaven, I learned a lesson. Since the ICW has very calm water almost all the way, I had left the TV and all the lamps up while we traveled. When cruising in the ocean, Gulf, Great Lakes, etc. where we could have rough water, I always put the TV and lamps on the floor so they couldn't fall off.

Thirty minutes out of Belhaven we ran aground going full speed at 18 knots in the Alligator canal. The TV and the lamps flew through the air; somehow, nothing was broken. The refrigerator door flew open and all the contents flew out. Magazines and all items on counter surfaces also became airborne.

We were very lucky to have so little damage. We had towing insurance with Boat U.S. and they pulled us off within 30 minutes. However, the lesson I learned is that when cruising, you should prepare the boat for rough water even if your course is anticipated to be very smooth.

Midway Marina (MM 49.5)
> #157 Coinjock Development Road
> Coinjock, NC 27923
> Phone: (252) 453-3625
> www.midwaymarina.com

Approach Depth	12'	Diesel Fuel	yes
Dockside Depth	10'	Mechanical Repairs	yes
Accepts Transients	yes	Ships Store	yes
Dockside Power	30,50	Showers	yes
Dockside Water	yes	Laundromat	yes
Gasoline	yes	Restaurant	no

Coinjock to Norfolk

The trip from Coinjock to Norfolk is 49 miles. Using the *Maptech Chart Kit,* follow the canal to the Currituck Sound and then to the North Landing River to the Albemarle and Chesapeake Canal, which has one lock. The canal continues where it connects with the South Elizabeth River. Follow the South Elizabeth River into Norfolk Harbor. The Waterside Marina is at Town Point at ICW SM 0.0.

The last few miles of the South Elizabeth River and Norfolk Harbor had the largest concentration of naval ships that I have ever seen. There were submarines, cruisers, destroyers, two carriers and many other types of Navy ships. I would guess that there were between 50 and 100 Navy ships there.

Norfolk

The Norfolk Waterfront at Town Point has been rebuilt similar to Baltimore Inner Harbor. The Rouse Company, who rebuilt Baltimore Inner Harbor, also rebuilt the Norfolk Waterfront. The Waterfront Marina is part of the complex, which includes 100 shops and restaurants. Just like Baltimore Inner Harbor, they often have free outside entertainment.

Waterside Marina
    333 Waterside Drive
    Norfolk, VA 23510
    Phone: (757) 625-2000
    www.waterwidemarina.com

Approach Depth	40'	Diesel Fuel	yes
Dockside Depth	20'	Mechanical Repairs	no
Accepts Transients	yes	Ships Store	yes
Dockside Power	30,50,100	Showers	yes
Dockside Water	yes	Laundromat	yes
Gasoline	no	Restaurant	yes

One of the many beautiful pre-Civil War homes
in Charleston, South Carolina

A treasure hunting boat docked at the
Heritage Plantation Marina, South Carolina

The B&B at the River Forest Marina
in Belhaven, North Carolina

A carrier docked in Norfolk Harbor

185

Norfolk to Avalon

Chesapeake & Delaware Bays

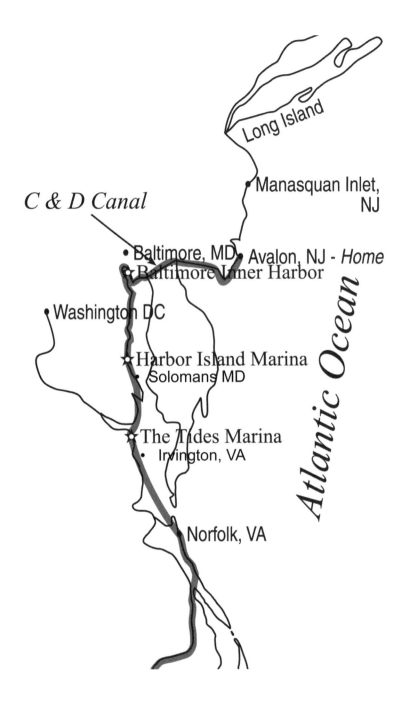

C & D Canal

Long Island

• Manasquan Inlet, NJ

• Baltimore, MD • Avalon, NJ - *Home*
• Baltimore Inner Harbor

• Washington DC

☆ Harbor Island Marina
• Solomans MD

☆ The Tides Marina
• Irvington, VA

• Norfolk, VA

Atlantic Ocean

Chapter 16

Norfolk to Avalon
Chesapeake and Delaware Bays

Destination	Marina	Statute Miles	Cumulative Miles
(Depart Norfolk)			
Irvington, VA	The Tides Marina	70	5123
Solomans, VA	Harbor Island Marina	70	5193
Tangier Island &			
Crisfield, MD	Somers Cove Marina		
Cambridge, MD	Cambridge Yacht Club Marina		
St. Michaels, MD	St. Michaels Yacht Club		
Annapolis, MD	The Yacht Basin Company		
Baltimore, MD	Baltimore Inner Harbor	80	5273
Chesapeake City, MD	Shafer's Marina		
(C & D Canal)			
Avalon, NJ	Home Port	137	5410

Charts Required:
> *Maptech ChartKit—Chesapeake & Delaware Bays*

Cruising Guide:
> *Waterway Guide—Mid-Atlantic*

(On the preceding page, the destinations where the author stayed are shown in bold type. These destinations are described in the following chapter. The other destinations are listed as intermediate ports if a shorter cruising day is desired. Check the cruising guide for information on intermediate ports.)

The Chesapeake Bay

The Chesapeake Bay is truly a cruising paradise, with 4,000 miles of coastline and countless destinations. The bay is 200 miles long and approximately 20 miles wide, with an average depth of 20 feet. The water changes from salt water in the southern bay to brackish water in mid-bay to fresh water in the northern bay. Destinations vary. There are large cities—such as Norfolk, Washington D.C., Baltimore, and Annapolis—small towns, such as St. Michaels, Cambridge, and Rockhall; and numerous gunkholes. The huge number of rivers and creeks that flow into the Chesapeake provide countless anchorages in quiet, protected water.

Since we keep our boat in Avalon, New Jersey, we can get to the Chesapeake in approximately 5 hours. Consequently, we have taken 8 different Chesapeake cruises; all were different.

Norfolk to Irvington, VA (Tides Inn)

Since the Chesapeake has a lot of shallow areas, I normally follow the blue course lines in the Chesapeake Chart Book as long as they are going where I want to go. I also use the GPS to guide me from waypoint to waypoint.

Tides Inn

Tides Inn is a four-star resort where you can stay on your boat and enjoy all their facilities. The Tides Inn has two golf courses, tennis courts, two restaurants, a sandy beach, and a large swimming pool area. This is a great place to stay for several days for a change of pace.

The Tides Marina
> 480 King Carter Drive
> Irvington, VA 22480
> Phone: (804) 438-5000
> www.tidesinn.com

Approach Depth	6'	Diesel Fuel	no
Dockside Depth	6'	Mechanical Repairs	no
Accepts Transients	yes	Ships Store	yes
Dockside Power	30,50	Showers	yes
Dockside Water	yes	Laundromat	yes
Gasoline	no	Restaurant	no

Tangier Island

Tangier Island in the Chesapeake Bay was first settled 300 years ago by the English. The 550 people who live there still have an old English accent.

The island has a small airport for private planes but is mainly connected to the mainland by ferry. Tangier Island did not have electricity until after World War II. The islanders make a living by crabbing, specializing in soft-shell crabs.

There is no formal local government; rather, order is maintained by family rule, town fathers, and the Methodist Church, the only church on the island. (Interestingly, in the Methodist Church's graveyard, stone caskets are above ground because the water level is only 2 feet below the surface.)

An island school covers kindergarten through 12th grade. The year we were there, our guide told us that their school had graduated nine students that year and all nine were accepted into college. The island has only one village, a look-alike for a New England fishing village.

Eleven miles north is Smith Island, which is very similar. The main difference between Smith Island and Tangier Island is that Smith Island is in Maryland and Tangier Island is in Virginia.

Crisfield, VA

Crisfield is known as the crab capital of the world. In fact, beside the state marina are grandstands from which spectators can watch the annual crab races.

The town was originally settled by farmers in the 1600s; by the 1800s it had become the oyster fishing center. However, as oystering declined over the last 40 years, the more abundant blue crab became the major business of Crisfield.

Crisfield is a nice place to visit on a boat because everything is within walking distance. There are a number of good restaurants where you can have the best crab cakes in the world.

Somers Cove Marina
715 Broadway
Crisfield, MO 21817
Phone: (410) 968-0925
www.dnr.maryland.gov/publiclands/eastern/somerscove.html

Approach Depth	10'	Diesel Fuel	yes
Dockside Depth	10'	Mechanical Repairs	no
Accepts Transients	yes	Ships Store	no

Dockside Power	30,50	Showers	yes
Dockside Water	yes	Laundromat	yes
Gasoline	yes	Restaurant	no

Cambridge, MD

Cambridge was founded in the 1600s and has been a seaport ever since. The marinas are located near Cambridge Creek. We stayed at the Cambridge Yacht Club, a very nice facility with a good restaurant. A few blocks from the Yacht Club is historic High Street, and the downtown shops are a few blocks beyond that. Clayton's Restaurant is a popular place to eat.

Cambridge Yacht Club Marina
　　1 Mill Street
　　Cambridge, MD 21613
　　Phone: (410) 228-2141

Approach Depth	8'	Diesel Fuel	no
Dockside Depth	8'	Mechanical Repairs	no
Accepts Transients	yes	Ships Store	no
Dockside Power	30,50	Showers	yes
Dockside Water	yes	Laundromat	no
Gasoline	yes	Restaurant	yes

St. Michaels, MD

St. Michaels, probably the most popular destination on the Eastern Shore, is a delightful town with many shops and restaurants as well as the Chesapeake Bay Maritime Museum. The museum, well worth a visit, includes a lighthouse that was moved to the museum as one of the exhibits.

There are two marinas: the St. Michaels Harbor Inn and the St. Michaels Town Dock Marina. Both have swimming pools and restaurants; however, the Town Dock Marina is a shorter walk to town.

St. Michaels Town Dock Marina
305 Mulberry Street
St. Michaels, MO 21663
Phone: (800) 678-8980
www.stmichaelsmarina.com

Approach Depth	10'	Diesel Fuel	yes
Dockside Depth	9'	Mechanical Repairs	no
Accepts Transients	yes	Ships Store	yes
Dockside Power	30,50	Showers	yes
Dockside Water	yes	Laundromat	yes
Gasoline	yes	Restaurant	yes

Annapolis, MD

Annapolis is my favorite boating destination. It has everything— great restaurants, entertainment, history, sightseeing, beautiful colonial buildings—and everything is walking distance from the marina. A water taxi takes you anywhere for one dollar.

Annapolis is the state capital of Maryland; the historic capital building is only a few blocks from the waterfront. Many of the streets around the capital are cobblestone, and the buildings are original from colonial times. The Naval Academy is adjacent and is well worth a tour.

We always stay at the Annapolis Yacht Basin [the Yacht Basin Company], which is next to the Annapolis Yacht Club and overlooks the Naval Academy. If you belong to a yacht club, the Annapolis Yacht Club will give you a guest pass so you can have dinner there. The Yacht Club dining room is on the top floor and overlooks the Annapolis Harbor, which is quite beautiful with many boats moored in the harbor.

On the other side of the marina is the Marriott Hotel, which has waterfront outdoor dining facing the famous "Ego Alley," a narrow strip of water with shops and restaurants on either side where people bring their boats into a dead end and then turn around and go back out.

The Yacht Basin Company
  2 Compromise Street
  Annapolis, MD 21401
  Phone: (4 1 0) 2 6 3 - 3 5 4 4
  www.yachtbasinco.com

Approach Depth	15'	Diesel Fuel	yes
Dockside Depth	15'	Mechanical Repairs	no
Accepts Transients	yes	Ships Store	yes
Dockside Power	30,50,100	Showers	yes
Dockside Water	yes	Laundromat	yes
Gasoline	yes	Restaurant	no

Baltimore Inner Harbor

Baltimore Inner Harbor is my second-favorite destination to Annapolis. You will want to stay in the Inner Harbor Marina of Baltimore, right in the Inner Harbor. The marina office and ships store is in the same building with the Rusty Scupper Restaurant. Since this destination is so popular, you will have to make reservations for the marina several weeks in advance. The Inner Harbor has many restaurants and hundreds of shops plus outside entertainment.

The National Aquarium is a "must see." A boat ride to historic Fells Point and Fort McHenry are also recommended. If you are a baseball fan, you are within walking distance to Camden Yards where the Baltimore Orioles play in what many say is the best baseball stadium in the country. Baltimore Inner Harbor also has an IMAX show and the frigate *Constellation*, launched in 1797, that you can visit.

Inner Harbor Marina of Baltimore
400 Key Highway
Baltimore, MD 21230
Phone: (410) 837-1834
www.baltimoreinnerharbormarinecenter.com

Approach Depth	40'	Diesel Fuel	yes
Dockside Depth	25'	Mechanical Repairs	no
Accepts Transients	yes	Ships Store	yes
Dockside Power	30,50	Showers	yes
Dockside Water	yes	Laundromat	yes
Gasoline	yes	Restaurant	yes

Chesapeake City (C & D Canal)

The C & D Canal originally opened in 1829 to link the Chesapeake Bay with the Delaware River. Chesapeake City was originally built to house the workers who built the canal. During the Civil War, Union forces were stationed here to make sure that the Confederate Army did not blow up the canal.

In the early 1900s the canal was rebuilt to eliminate the locks and to permit large boats to pass through. Today, the 12-mile-long canal is 450 feet wide and 35 feet deep, which permits large ocean-going ships to transit.

Free dockage is available at the government wharf in Chesapeake City; however, it is better to anchor out. The Bayard House Restaurant is the place to eat, with a view of the canal. On the opposite side of the canal from Chesapeake City is Schaefer's Canal House, which has transients' slips, fuel, and a large restaurant.

Schaefer's Market and Marina
208 Bank Street
Chesapeake City, MD 21915
Phone: (410) 885-2204

Approach Depth	36'	Diesel Fuel	yes
Dockside Depth	14'	Mechanical Repairs	no
Accepts Transients	yes	Ships Store	yes
Dockside Power	30,50	Showers	yes
Dockside Water	yes	Laundromat	no
Gasoline	yes	Restaurant	yes

Chesapeake Bay to Cape May, New Jersey

The trip from Chesapeake City to Cape May, New Jersey is 69 statute miles.   Height restriction on the Cape May Canal is 55 feet.   The Canyon Club Marina is on your left immediately after passing under the bridge.

Cape May, New Jersey

Cape May, New Jersey probably has the largest number of Victorian houses in any one place.   Many of the Victorian homes are B & B's offering bed and breakfast in a Victorian setting.

If you are staying in the Canyon Club Marina, take a taxi to the boardwalk area and take a leisurely walk up and down the many streets with nothing but Victorian gingerbread houses. Another popular way to see this unique town is by horse drawn carriage.

Cape May is known for its many good restaurants. Some of the best restaurants are the Washington Inn, Peaches Sunset, the Ebbett Room in the Virginia Hotel, and the Mad Batter.

Canyon Club Marina
900 Ocean Drive
Cape May, NJ 08204
Phone: (609) 884-0199
www.canyonclubmarina.com

Approach Depth	6'	Diesel Fuel	yes
Dockside Depth	6'	Mechanical Repairs	yes
Accepts Transients	yes	Ships Store	yes
Dockside Power	30,50	Showers	yes
Dockside Water	yes	Laundromat	no
Gasoline	yes	Restaurant	no

This photo was taken 7/7/97
Between Norfolk and Irvington on southern portion of
Chesapeake Bay

Nittany Navy at Baltimore Inner Harbor

Tides Inn on the Rappahannock River

CHAPTER 17

OTHER WATERWAYS

An alternate to the author's route would be to travel north from New York Harbor to the St. Lawrence River at Sorel, transiting Lake Champlain, Riviere Richelieu and Chambly Canal. Travel the St. Lawrence to Montreal to Lake Ontario or west on the Ottawa River to the Rideau Waterway to Kingston on the northeast shore of Lake Ontario. From Kingston travel through the Bay of Quinte to Trenton on the Trent Severn Waterway. The Trent Severn Waterway is a short cut between Lake Ontario and Georgian Bay part of Lake Huron. Once in Georgian Bay, you must make a decision to run the bay, open water, or take the scenic inside route.

The northern part of Lake Huron is the North Channel, a pristine waterway bordered to the south by Manitoulin Island (the largest fresh-water island in the world). At the west end of the North Channel the journey passes through De Tour Passage into Lake Huron, heading toward the Straits of Mackinac (pronounced Mackinaw), where the author's trip continues.

Vessels with greater heights than listed below can enter/exit the Great Lakes via the St. Lawrence Seaway and Welland Canal.

Bridge Restrictions	Feet
Illinois Waterway	19.1
Entrance Chicago Lock	17.0
New York State Canal System	20.5
Buffalo to Lyons	15.5
Champlain Canal	15.5
(Depending on local conditions could be 17.0)	

Draft Restrictions	Feet
Trent Severn	5.0
(Actual depth 6 feet)	

Length of Vessel	Feet
Trent Severn	100.0

Beam of Vessel	Feet
Trent Severn	24.0

Reference Material
 Waterway Guides:
  Great Lakes
  Northern
  Mid-Atlantic
  Southern

<u>Reference Material (continued)</u>

Quimby's Guide

Ports O'Call:

Lake Michigan

Lake Huron

Lake Erie

Lake Ontario

River Cruise Guides:

A Cruising Guide from Lake Michigan to Kentucky Lake

Cumberland River

Skipper Bob—a dozen guides that cover various sections and topics of the Circle Route

Tennessee River

Tenn-Tom Nitty-Gritty

Coast Pilots, Sailing Directions, Small Craft Guides

NOAA Charts

THE FOLLOWING TABLE DEPICTS THE AUTHOR'S ACTUAL ROUTE

River System: Lake Michigan to Gulf of Mexico via Tombigbee	Mile Mark	Cumulative Miles
Chicago River	326.7	
Calumet Sag	333.5	
	303.5	
Illinois	290.0	
Illinois	286.0	
Illinois	273.7	59.8
Illinois	271.5	
Illinois	244.6	
Illinois	231.0	
Illinois	196.1	137.4
Illinois	157.8	
Illinois	97.5	236.0
Illinois	80.2	
Upper Mississippi	217.9	333.5
Upper Mississippi	212.4	
Upper Mississippi	200.8	
Upper Mississippi	185.0	
Upper Mississippi	122.5	

READ ACROSS THE ROWS

Facility	Locks
	Chicago Lock (1)
Calumet Harbor	
Junction: Chicago Sanitary & Ship Canal with Calumet Sag Channel	
	Lockport L&D (2)
	Brandon Road L&D (3)
Harborside Marina	
	Dresden L&D (4)
	Marseilles L&D (5)
	Starved Rock L&D (6)
Henry Harbor Landing & Inn	
	Peoria L&D (7)
Rivers Edge Boat Club	
	La Grange L&D (8)
Upper Mississippi Junction	
My River Home Harbor*	
	Melvin Price L&D (9)
	Chain of Rocks Canal L&D (10)
Marina de Gabouri**	

*   My River Home Harbor: Alton Marina (Mile 202.9 LDB) is the preferred marina along this portion of the waterway.

**   Marina de Gabouri is probably not accessible. (Silted in.)

River System: Lake Michigan to Gulf of Mexico via Tombigbee	Mile Mark	Cumulative Miles
Upper Mississippi	117.3	
Upper Mississippi	1.2	
Ohio River	981.0	551.4
Ohio River	962.6	
Ohio River	935.0	597.9
Ohio River	935.0	
Tennessee River	22.4	
Ohio River	923.0	609.9
Cumberland River	30.6	
Cumberland River	31.7	641.0
Tennessee River	2.5	644.1
Tennessee River	25.5	
Tennessee River	115.5	
Tennessee River	206.7	
Tennessee River	215.2	833.8
Tombigbee Waterway	450.0	
Tombigbee Waterway	448.7	
Tombigbee Waterway	411.9	

Facility	Locks
Kaskaskia River Mouth	
Anchorage*	Cairo Highway Bridge
Ohio River Mouth	
	Lock 53 (11)
	Lock 52 (12)
Tennessee River Mouth	
	Kentucky Lock (13-A)
Cumberland River Mouth	
	Barclay L&D (13-B)
Green Turtle Bay	
Barclay Canal	
Barclay Canal & Tennessee River	
Cuba Landing Marina	
	Pickwick Landing Lock (14)
Entrance Tombigbee Waterway	
Yellow Creek	
Aqua Yacht Harbor	
	Jamie Whitten L&D [formerly Bay Springs Lock] (15)

* After this anchorage, the author traveled up the Ohio River, passing the Tennessee River Junction, to purchase gas, then backtracked to the Tennessee. That fuel stop no longer exists. The recommended route after entering the Ohio River is to travel to the Cumberland River, through the Barclay Lock & Dam to Green Turtle Marina. Then continue to the Tennessee River via the Barclay Canal.

River System: Lake Michigan to Gulf of Mexico via Tombigbee	Mile Mark	Cumulative Miles
Tombigbee Waterway	406.7	
Tombigbee Waterway	398.4	
Tombigbee Waterway	391.0	
Tombigbee Waterway	377.0	
Tombigbee Waterway	376.3	
Tombigbee Waterway	371.1	
Tombigbee Waterway	357.5	
Tombigbee Waterway	307.4	977.1
Tombigbee Waterway	334.7	
Tombigbee Waterway	306.8	
Tombigbee Waterway	266.1	
Tombigbee Waterway	217.0	
Lower Black Warrior	216.7	1,068.4
Lower Black Warrior	213.2	
Lower Black Warrior	118.9	1,166.2
Lower Black Warrior	116.6	
Mobile Bay	0.0	1,285.1
Mobile Bay: Dog River		1,300.0

Facility	Locks
	G.V. "Sonny" Montgomery Lock (E) (16)
	John Rankin Lock (D) (17)
	Fulton Lock (C) (18)
Smithville Marina	
	Glover Wilkins Lock (B) (19)
	Amory Lock (A) (20)
	Aberdeen L&D (21)
Marina Cove	
	John C. Stennis L&D (23)
	Tom Bevill L&D (23)
	Howell Heflin L&D (24)
Junction: Black Warrior River	
Demopolis Yacht Basin	
	Demopolis L&D (25)
Lady's Landing*	
	Coffeeville L&D (26)
Grand Mariner Marina	

*   Lady's Landing no longer exists. Bobby's Fish Camp is the place to fuel and lay over.

BICK'S DESTINATIONS AND CUMULATIVE MILEAGE

Leg	Day	Chapter	Date 1996	Depart	MM
I	1	5	06/07	Avalon, NJ	
	2		06/08	Manasquan	
	3		06/09	Tarrytown	
	4		06/10	Troy	
	5		06/11	Fultonville	
	6		06/12	Rome	
	7		06/13	Baldwinsville	
	8		06/14	Fairport, NY	
	9-11		06/15	Lockport	
	12	6	06/18	Buffalo	
	13-15		06/19	Erie	
	16		06/22	Cleveland	
	17		06/23	Sandusky	
	18-21		06/24	Put-In-Bay	
	22	7	06/28	Detroit	
	23		06/29	Port Huron	
	24		06/30	Harbor Beach	
	25		07/01	Harrisville	
	26-28		07/02	Cheboygan	
	29	8	07/05	Mackinac Island	
	30-32		07/06	Petoskey	
	33		07/09	Charlevoix	
	34		07/10	Frankfort	
	35		07/11	Holland	
	36-37		07/12	Benton Harbor	327.0
	38-41		07/14	Chicago	273.7
II	42	9	09/10	Wilmington	196.1

Read Across Rows

Arrive	Marina	Miles	Cumulative Miles
Manasquan Inlet, NJ	Brielle Yacht Club	96	96
Tarrytown, NY	Tarrytown Marina	63	159
Troy, NY	Troy Town Dock	109	268
Fultonville, NY	Poplars Inn & Marina	48	316
Rome, NY	Riverside Marina	66	382
Baldwinsville, NY	Coopers Marina	58	440
Fairport, NY	Town Dock	74	514
Lockport, NY	Goehle Municipal	74	588
Buffalo, NY	Erie Basin Marina	34	622
Erie, PA	Erie Yacht Club	82	704
Cleveland, OH	Old River Yacht Club	101	805
Sandusky, OH	Cedar Point Marina	64	869
Put-In-Bay, OH	Boardwalk Marina	21	890
Detroit, MI	Keans Detroit Yacht Harbor	52	942
Port Huron, MI	Municipal Marina	50	992
Harbor Beach, MI	Harbor Beach Marina	55	1047
Harrisville, MI	Harrisville City Dock	55	1102
Cheboygan, MI	Walstrom Marina	91	1193
Mackinac Island, MI	Mackinac Island Marina	14	1207
Petoskey, MI	Petoskey Municipal	50	1257
Charlevoix, MI	Northwest Marina	15	1272
Frankfort, MI	Jacobson Marina	67	1339
Holland, MI	Eldean Shipyard	114	1453
Benton Harbor, MI	Riverview 1000	41	1494
Chicago, IL	Burnham Park	53	1547
Wilmington, IL	Harborside Marina	55	1602
Henry, IL	Henry Harbor Marina	78	1680

BICK'S DESTINATIONS AND CUMULATIVE MILEAGE

Leg	Day	Chapter	Date 1996	Depart	MM
II	43	9	09/11	Henry, IL	97.5
	44		09/12	Browning, IL	212.4
	45		09/13	Portage Des Sioux	122.5
	46		09/14	St. Genevieve	98.0
	47-48		09/15	Cairo	31.7
	49		09/16	Grand Rivers	115.5
	50-54		09/17	Waverly	448.7
	55	10	09/23	Iuka	411.9
	56		09/24	Bay Springs	307.4
	57		09/25	Carrolton	216.7
	58		09/26	Demopolis	80.0
	59-62		09/27	Jackson	7.0
	63	11	10/03	Mobile	
	64-69		10/04	Biloxi	
Leg	Day		Date 1997	Depart	MM
II	70-71		01/17	New Orleans	
	72		01/19	Biloxi	
	73-75		01/20	Pensacola	227.0
	76		01/23	Destin	290.0
	77-79		01/24	Panama City	
	80		01/27	Carrabelle	
	81	12	01/28	Cedar Key	
	82		01/29	Tarpon Springs	77.4
	83-87		01/30	Longboat Key	
	88		02/04	Boca Grande	
	89-95		02/05	Marco Island	1243

READ ACROSS ROWS

Arrive	Marina	Miles	Cumulative Miles
Browning, IL	Rivers Edge Boat Club	99	1779
Portage des Sioux	My River Home	104	1883
St. Genevieve, MO	Marina de Gabori	90	1973
Cairo, IL	Anchorage	121	2094
Grand Rivers, KY	Green Turtle Bay	83	2177
Waverly, KY	Cuba Landing	92	2269
Iuka, MS	Aqua Yacht Harbor	104	2373
Bay Springs, AL	Smithville Marina	72	2445
Carrolton, AL	Marina Cove	69	2514
Demopolis, AL	Demopolis Yacht Basin	91	2605
Jackson, AL	Lady's Landing	137	2742
Mobile, AL	Grand Mariner Marina	87	2829
Biloxi, MS	Point Cadet Marina	85	2914
New Orleans	Orleans Marina	106	3020
Arrive	Marina	Miles	Cumulative Miles
Biloxi, MS	Point Cadet Marina	106	3126
Pensacola, FL	Harbor Village	97	3223
Destin, FL	Sandestin's Baytowne	30	3253
Panama City	Bay Point Marina	45	3298
Carrabelle, FL	The Moorings	80	3378
Cedar Key, FL	Municipal Dock	120	3498
Tarpon Springs, FL	Port Tarpon Marina	60	3558
Longboat Key, FL	Longboat Key Moorings	65	3623
Boca Grande, FL	Millers Marina	43	3666
Marco Island, FL	Marco River Marina	65	3731
Key West, FL	The Galleon Marina	98	3829

BICK'S DESTINATIONS AND CUMULATIVE MILEAGE

Leg	Day	Chapter	Date 1997	Depart	MM
II	96	13	02/12	Key West	1193
	97		02/13	Marathon	1134
	98		02/14	Key Largo	1064
	99-104		02/15	Fort Lauderdale	1039
	105-106		02/21	Delray Beach	1020
III	107-108	14	06/19	West Palm Beach	952
	109		06/21	Vero Beach	878
	110-111		06/22	Titusville	778
	112		06/24	St. Augustine	684
	113-114		06/25	Jekyll Island	582
	115-117	15	06/27	Savannah	469
	118		06/30	Charleston	395
	119		07/01	Georgetown	320
	120-121		07/02	Southport	204
	122		07/04	Morehead City	136
	123		07/05	Belhaven	49
	124		07/06	Coinjock	0
	125	16	07/07	Norfolk	
	126		07/08	Irvington	
	127-128		07/09	Solomans	
	129		07/11	Baltimore	

READ ACROSS ROWS

Arrive	Marina	Miles	Cumulative Miles
Marathon, FL	Faro Blanco Bayside	50	3879
Key Largo, FL	Gilbert's Holiday Island	59	3938
Fort Lauderdale	Bahia Mar Marina	50	3988
Delray Beach	Delray Beach Yacht Club	25	4013
West Palm Beach	Rybovich Spencer	20	4033
Vero Beach, FL	Complete Yacht Service	68	4101
Titusville, FL	Titusville Municipal Marina	74	4175
St. Augustine, FL	St. Augustine Municipal	100	4275
Jekyll Island, GA	Jekyll Harbor Marina	94	4369
Savannah, GA	Savannah Bend Marina	102	4471
Charleston, SC	Charleston City Marina	113	4584
Georgetown, SC	Heritage Plantation Marina	74	4658
Southport, NC	Blue Water	75	4733
Morehead City	Morehead City Yacht Basin	116	4849
Belhaven, NC	River Forest Marina	68	4917
Coinjock, NC	Midway Marina	87	5004
Norfolk, VA	Waterside Marina	49	5053
Irvington, VA	Tides Inn	70	5123
Solomans, MD	Harbor Island Marina	70	5193
Baltimore, MD	Baltimore Inner Harbor	80	5273
Avalon, NJ	Home Port	137	5410

Following is a list of charts commonly used by operators of pleasure craft planning to "circumnavigate" or cruise in waterways of the Eastern US and Canada. In northern waters the Trent Severn, Georgian Bay, and North Channel (all Canadian waters), is often the preferred route. Taking into consideration height, draft, time limits, and additional restrictions, other routes—such as running through Lake Ontario, Lake Erie, and Lake Huron—are an option.

Lake Michigan to Gulf of Mexico via Inland Rivers:
  Illinois Waterway (Lake Michigan to junction Upper Mississippi River)
  Upper Mississippi (Minneapolis to junction of Ohio River)
  Ohio River: Foster, KY to Cairo, IL
  Cumberland River (Recommended to avoid delay at Kentucky Lock on
    Tennessee River)
  Tennessee River (Barclay Canal to Pickwick, TN)
  Tombigbee Waterway (Pickwick, TN to Demopolis, AL)
  Lower Black Warrior River (Demopolis, AL to Mobile Bay)
  11376 Mobile Bay Chart

Mobile Bay, AL to Florida:
  11378 ICW Chart: Dauphin Island to Santa Rosa Sound
  11385 ICW Chart: Santa Rosa Sound to West Bay
  Maptech ChartKit Region 8: Florida West Coast & Keys (Includes
    Okeechobee Waterway)

Miami, FL to Oswego, NY via New York State Canal System (NYSCS):
  11467, 11472, 11485, 11489 Miami, FL to St. Simons, GA
  Maptech ChartKit: Norfolk, VA to Jacksonville, FL
  Maptech ChartKit: Chesapeake & Delaware Bays
  12316 & 12324 Cape May, NJ to Sandy Hook, NY
  12327 New York Harbor (Small Scale Chart: Pass through)

Embassy Chart #4: Hudson River
14786 New York State Canal System

swego, NY to Entrance of Trent Severn Waterway:
14802 & 14803 Crossing Lake Ontario to Bay of Quinte
2006, 2007, 2011, 2069 Telegraph Narrows & Bay of Quinte (Canada)

ent Severn Waterway:
2021, 2022, 2023, 2024, 2025, 2028, 2029 Trenton, ON to Port Severn, ON

eorgian Bay (Inside Route):
2202, 2203, 2204 Port Severn, ON to Killarney, ON

orth Channel:
2205, 2206, 2207, 2251, 2257, 2258, 2259, 2268, 2299

etour Passage and Straits of Mackinac: (Always pronounced "Mackinaw")
14882, 14881

ke Michigan:
Maptech ChartKit Region 13: Lake Michigan
        OR
Richardsons' Chartbook: Lake Michigan
        OR
Individual Charts may be selected.

<u>ALTERNATE TO TRENT SEVERN, GEORGIAN BAY, NORTH CHANNEL</u>

At Oswego, NY travel west (on Lake Ontario), using Richardsons' Chartbook: Lake Ontario or individual NOAA Charts, to the Welland Canal or continue west (from Lyons, NY) on the NYSCS to Lake Erie (maximum overhead 15½ feet), then to the Detroit River, Lake St. Clair, St. Clair River to Lake Huron to the Straits of Mackinac. Richardsons' Chartbook: Lake Erie is often used to transit Lake Erie. This chart extends to Port Huron, MI. Waterproof Charts number 74 & 75 cover Lake Huron and Straits of Mackinac (did you remember, "Mackinaw"?).

Refer to chart catalogs in order to follow these routes. It is important to select charts from Canadian Hydrographic Catalogs for travel in Canadian waters and US Catalogs for travel in United States. Canadian law requires "official" charts; therefore, Canadian Hydrographic Charts are required in Canadian waters.

Also, refer to the catalogs for *additional alternate routes:* for example, travel through Lake Champlain, Richelieu River (to Montreal), Ottawa River, and the Rideau Waterway into Lake Ontario and enter Telegraph Narrows on the way to the Trent Severn.

Contact me, Laura Cannell, and I will advise and assist you in selecting proper guides and charts for the route of your choice.

Marine Navigation, Inc.
613 South La Grange Road

La Grange, IL 60525-6724
Bu: 708 352-0606 Fax: 708 352-2170
e-mail: mnilaura@ameritech.net
e-mail: laura@marinenavigationinc.com
www.marinenavigationinc.com
"You'd be lost without us!" ˢᵐ